A Proud Tradition

Britain declared war on Germany on 4th August 1914. The causes of the war were complex, involving the growth of German imperialism, Austrian dislike of Serbia and a series of treaties and alliances dating back to the nineteenth century. But the immediate catalyst, so far as Britain was concerned, was German violation of Belgian neutrality, of which Britain was a guarantor.

The British regular army at that time was extremely small compared to Germany's, and the men in the second line of defence, the Territorials, were not compelled to serve overseas. In the event many of them volunteered, but by that time Lord Kitchener, newly in charge at the War Office, had appealed for the "first 100,000". At Lord Derby's instigation two "Pals" battalions were formed in Liverpool, the idea being that men who enlisted together would serve together, and on 28th August Manchester employers met and resolved to raise and equip a battalion from the city's offices and warehouses. The devastating casualty figures that the war would produce were not foreseen at the time and no-one anticipated how few of these Pals would come back. Eventually eight battalions were formed in Manchester; Albert's brother Tom enlisted in the 1st City Pals, and Albert joined the 4th, who had their first parade on 16th September. The title was changed to 19th (Service) Battalion on 3rd December.

When he volunteered, Albert was working as a clerk, serving writs for a firm near Ardwick - a job he was good at, but hated. However, he had been brought up in the knowledge that his grandfather, David Andrews, had been one of the survivors of the Charge of the Light Brigade. The family still have his spurs and Albert's father was christened Albert Edward Cardigan Andrews, after Lord Cardigan, who led the charge. Perhaps the sense of adventure which prompted both boys to join up on the same day came from their distinguished ancestor.

A photograph taken in the signal box at London Road Station. Albert Edward Cardigan Andrews, Albert's father, is on the right

Albert's grandfather, David Andrews of the 11th Hussars

Albert's parents were 25 years old when he was born on 19th March 1891. His mother, Sarah Ann (Sall), had been a mill girl, employed since she learned to wind bobbins at ten years old. At the time of their marriage in 1886 Albert senior gave his occupation as grocer, but when Tom was born in 1893 he was working as a railway storesman. The two boys came from a large family; the others were Florrie, Fred, George Edward, Lily, who died when she was twelve years old and twins who died at birth. Both Albert and Tom were born at 9 William Street, West Gorton, but the family later moved to 48 Church Lane and were living there when the boys enlisted.

Basic Training

Belle Vue and Heaton Park

An informal group at Heaton Park, with Albert Andrews in civvies, front left

Monday 7 Sept 1914: I joined the 4th City Pals of the Manchester Regiment, my brother Tom having joined the 1st the same day. The 1st, 2nd, 3rd and 4th Pals were better known later as the 16th, 17th, 18th and 19th Battalions of the Manchester Regiment and comprised the 90th Brigade.

My first few weeks in the Army were spent at the City [Exhibition] Hall, Manchester, where we were formed up and did a little drill in our civilian clothes. I was in 13th Section, 8th Platoon, B Company, under Sergeant Bush, Lieutenant Mather and Captain Birley, Colonel Heywood being in command and Colonel Lloyd second-in-command.

Sep to Nov 1914: We were moved to Belle Vue Gardens, Manchester, doing squad drill from 9.00am to 4.30pm [4.00pm]. By this time we had our uniform, navy blue with red piping and a peaked hat like a marine's. In October [28th] our Colonel Heywood died [of pneumonia] and Colonel Kettlewell was appointed our Colonel [19th November].

30 Nov 1914: We were moved into huts in Heaton Park and started soldiering in earnest! From 6.00am until 7.00pm we did running, physical drill, section drill, platoon drill and company drill, with a night march after tea and a long route march once a week. I got two days CB at Heaton Park for my first crime in the Army - not saluting an officer. I hadn't seen him as it happened, but all I got was, "Keep your eyes open and look." The basic recruit course was completed by Christmas, and from then until April 1915 we did musketry, bayonet fighting, extended order drill and lectures.

B Company at dinner, Heaton Park

All the 90th Brigade were stationed at Heaton Park and our packs and equipment were inspected by our Brigadier General H C E Westropp, Lord Derby and General MacKinnon [Commander-in-Chief, Western Command, 1910-15].

[21 Mar] 1915: Just before we left Heaton Park we were inspected by Lord Kitchener. The streets of Manchester were crowded to see us do the march past from the camp five miles away to the Manchester Town Hall. The streets were lined with people and the City itself was packed. It was quite a great occasion for Manchester that day.

Part of 14 Platoon, D Company, 16th Manchesters. Tom Andrews is on the right, with his hands on the shoulders of the man in front

Belton Park, Grantham

[24] April 1915: From Heaton Park we were moved to Belton Park, Grantham, now in the 30th Division with General Fry in command. The Division was made up of our Brigade, the 90th, all Manchester lads; the 91st, all Manchester lads and the 89th Brigade, which was the Liverpool Pals, the County Palatine Artillery and a Battalion of South Lancashires as Pioneers.

One day we would do musketry, physical drill and so on, and the next day would be a Battalion day. This means the Battalion goes and does a long march, makes an attack and comes back again under the Colonel. The day after might be

The City Battalions marching through Cheetham Hill for the inspection by Lord Kitchener in Albert Square

19th (Service) Battalion Manchester Regiment.

"B" COMPANY.

Officer Commanding Company - Capt. H. KENNEDY BIRLEY *
Second in Command - - - Capt. C. Joyce *
Company Sergeant Major - - GRAYBURN, A. H. *
Company Quartermaster Sergeant - BUSH, G. W.

* *Not on photograph*

PLATOON NO. VIII.

Platoon Commander - - - - 2nd Lieut. E. W. MAWDSLEY.
Platoon Sergeant - - - - - WILSON, L. E.

Roll No.	Rank	Name
11857	L.-Sergt.	HUNTER, C. A.
11876	Corporal	LEAVER, H. C.
11569	L.-Corpl.	HARMAMAN, J.
11754	,,	BRANDRETH, ARTHUR.
11753	Private	BRANDRETH, ALBERT.
11899	,,	ANDREWS, A. W.
11729	,,	ALLEN, F.
11737	,,	BARLOW, H.
11742	,,	BECKETT, F.
11734	,,	BAILLIE, W.
11760	,,	BROOKES, W.
11805	,,	BAGALEY, E. G.
11761	,,	BROWN, E.
11743	,,	BENNETT, F. H.
11738	Private	BARNES, T.
11747	,,	BINKS, F. R.
12527	,,	BRIERLEY, J. H.
11736	,,	BARLOW, H.
11763	,,	BRYCE, F.
11768	,,	BROWNBILL, R. H
11776	,,	COOPER, F. G.
11781	,,	CROOKS, S.
11779	,,	COTTAM, A.
11805	,,	EVANS, F.
11802	,,	ELLIS, P. W.
11803	,,	ENGLAND, R. H.
11869	,,	FURNESS, R.
11813	,,	GIBBONS, W.
11824	Private	HALL, W.
11834	,,	HIGHTON, W.
11832	,,	HEYWOOD, R.
11843	,,	HOLLOS, F.
12619	,,	HOLLOS, E.
11848	,,	HOPWOOD, N.
11836	,,	HILTON, L.
11847	,,	HOLT, J.
11871	,,	LAMB, J. H.
11894	,,	MORTON, H. R.
12526	,,	MCNICHOLL, J. W.
12594	,,	MOTTERSHEAD, S. S.
11977	,,	NUTTALL, N.
12525	,,	ROBINSON, A.
11925	,,	SCHOLES, P.
11935	,,	STROMBERG, H. C.
11926	,,	SIDEBOTTOM, A.
11984	,,	THORPE, H.
11955	,,	WHITFIELD, G.
11981	,,	WHEATCROFT, F. H.
11954	,,	WHEATCROFT, S.
11956	,,	WHITEHEAD, J.

The following were not present when the Platoon Photograph was taken,

Roll No.	Rank	Name
11899	Corporal	OLLERENSHAW, H.
12596	Private	BROWN, G. B.
11757	,,	BRINDLE, H.
11796	Private	DOLAN, L.
11932	,,	SMITH, H.
11890	,,	MORAN, J.
12523	Private	FARRELL, J. W.
11856	,,	HULME, J. H.
11877	,,	LINGARD, J. M.

No.8 Platoon, B Company of the 19th Manchesters at Grantham. The photograph and list of names are taken from the Manchester City Battalions Book of Honour, 1917. Albert Andrews is fourth from the right on the back row. The platoon commander, 2/Lt E W Mawdsley, is in the middle of the second row from the front. He is flanked by Sgt Wilson and CQMS Bush

a Brigade day - the same thing but with the whole Brigade under the Brigadier and then a Divisional day, with the Divisional General directing the attack. This is how we spent the summer of 1915 up to the end of August.

19th Manchesters in Heaton Park: Machine Gun Section

Our training was from 10 to 12 hours per day, very stiff and at times tried the best of us. For instance, one day in June we had our breakfast at 6.00am, marched to Belvoir Castle, did a two mile attack and arrived back at 5.00pm, not having had any food since breakfast. The distance covered in marching alone was 25 miles with full pack, and the last ten miles of that was in a heavy storm.

But we used to visit Nottingham every time we had the chance at a weekend, and we went for cycle rides all over the place. I visited Nottingham, Newark, Sleaford, [Great] Ponton, Belvoir Castle and several smaller places while I was there. After one trip to Lincoln my pal Furness and I had a narrow escape. We left Lincoln about 9.00pm as we had to be in by midnight, but our bicycle lamps went out on the way back and we got completely lost. We eventually got back to camp about 5.00am and we had to be on parade at six! We got into bed to make the sergeant think we had been there all night, and made the excuse that we had forgotten to give in our passes the night before. We got away with it, but next morning the sergeant threatened to get the band to wake me, not a bugle!

19th Manchesters in Heaton Park: bayonet lessons

Another part of our training at Grantham was digging trenches at Willoughby, about 7 [17] miles from camp. We went there every day and when they were complete we spent two days and nights in them. Of course it had to rain every day! It was a common thing to come back to Grantham wet through three days out of the week. In one week's marching alone we did 12 miles on Monday, 21 Tuesday, 15 Wednesday, 25 Thursday and 10 Friday, making a total of 83 miles in five days and attacks each day.

[15 Jun] 1915: About this time our Colonel Kettlewell retired due to ill health. He sent us a message to say how sorry he was to leave us and that his parting message to us was one word, "Discipline" - no Battalion or Army could be a success without it. Brigadier Westropp also retired [2 September], saying he would follow the work of the Brigade always, as he had trained us from recruits. In place of Colonel Kettlewell, who was a great soldier and a grand old man, we had Sir H B Hill, Bart, who proved to us later what a great soldier he was.

By this time our Platoon Officer had left us, he being appointed junior Captain to our Company. Our new Platoon Officer was named Mawdsley, a thorough officer and a gentleman. Our Platoon were the best shots in the Battalion, for which he deserves credit. Every man tried his best for him, he was so good to us. The firing course consisted of firing at 100 yards, 5 rounds grouping; 10 rounds, 200 yards; 5 rounds, 500 yards and 5 rounds at 600 yards. We had to know every part of a rifle and what it was for and we had to be able to load 15 rounds and get them off in one minute, usually called "the mad minute". Our Company commander examined every man himself. We were taught observation, bridge building and knot tying as well, but the firing course was the most interesting of all.

For bayonet training we did plenty of jumping into trenches, sticking sacks placed in them and sacks hung up. I never seemed to be satisfied unless I sent one of these hanging sacks up with such a dig that I broke the cord.

Every Saturday at 12 noon we had tent and kit inspections. All

tables, forms and floors had to be scrubbed, the windows and stove cleaned and all rifles laid on the table cleaned, ready for the Colonel to pick any one up and inspect it. Each man's kit had to be set out on his bed in the same way. For these inspections the Colonel would be followed by the Adjutant, Captain, Platoon Officer, Platoon Sergeant and Regimental Police - quite a procession!

In addition to these we had special inspections from time to time by VIPs, including General Sir Archibald Murray, General Paget, General Hamilton, General MacKinnon and General Fry, our Divisional Commander. I remember General Fry asking me when I had had my hair cut.
"Last week, Sir."
"How much did you pay?"
"Threepence, Sir."
He then turned round to our

19th Manchesters on a route march near Grantham in May 1915. Top: The midday meal

Colonel and said, "Tell that barber he must cut hair for 1d or clear out." The Colonel tried to explain that the barber was a civilian, but, "That's enough!" replied the General. "1d or clear out - my orders. I am in command here!"

Sports were held which included horse-racing, boxing, bayonet fighting, running and football, with medals being given to the champion Battalion team. The Oldham Prize Band had enlisted in a body in their Battalion; the 16th, 17th and 18th Manchesters had a brass band; our Battalion, the 19th, a bugle band and then there was the Divisional Orchestra, about 40 strong. All the best musicians in the Division were in this band, which used to play every Saturday afternoon and was worth going a long way to hear.

I had a weekend leave and four days from Grantham, but we always had a good many friends from Manchester at the weekend. With 8,000 Manchesters there and 20,000 Lancashire lads in all, the railway found it worth while to run excursions from Manchester to Grantham. My own mother and sister stayed there several weeks and my father came once for a weekend.

All in all we had a very hard training but plenty of fun, and the people of Grantham quite changed their opinion of us. We were treated very coolly at first because we were from Manchester, but they were very sorry when we were going and a good many were up early in the morning to see us march past.

Larkhill Camp, Salisbury Plain

[7 Sep] 1915: The first week in September 1915 the Division was ordered to move to Salisbury Plain. We left Belton Camp about 5.00am, our bugle band playing the Last Post in front of the guard room. The train left Grantham about seven and arrived at Amesbury at 4.00pm, from where we marched to Larkhill, our new camp. Here the training was even more rigorous. For

General Fry

instance, one day in our third week there we paraded at 6.30am and did an hour's running and training before breakfast. Then the Battalion marched off 12 miles, did an attack and marched 12 miles back for tea. At 8.00pm we paraded again for another attack by night which involved

19th Manchesters bugle band

about 15 miles marching. When we got back to camp at 2.00am, the Captain ordered an inspection of our water bottles before we were dismissed and any man who had not a full water bottle had his name taken. The punishment for these men, after drill the next evening, was to march the five miles to the Captain's house at Amesbury with full water bottles. The Captain's wife had given us all small presents the week before; these the fellows threw into the front garden of the house, they were so disgusted with the Captain's treatment.

On the Monday of the following week we attacked a small village called Shrewton about 7 miles from camp and on the Tuesday marched a few miles further for another attack. On Wednesday we went further still and attacked again. It rained very hard this day and our Battalion fought a rearguard action for two miles, covering the Division as it was retiring. Thursday was the same again and by Friday morning we were all feeling the after effects of this hard work with full pack and rifle all the time; some of the fellows were hardly able to put their feet to the floor. It was raining and we all hoped it would keep on so as to give us a bit of a rest, but we were out of luck, we had to turn out. I think about 100 men fell out in the first 7 miles, unable to stick it any longer. I myself, never having fallen out of a march, kept on.

On Saturday we did not go far and after this attack our Brigadier formed us up and spoke to us. He said we had had a very hard week of it. Marching alone, we had covered 136 miles and over rough ground, but at the front we would have to do much more. For instance, he said, one brigade in the retreat from Mons covered 224 miles in the same time. I know when we arrived back that afternoon I had done enough for one week and lay on my bed for a few hours! Salisbury was only about 10 miles from Larkhill, but on the Sunday after church parade I caught the bus there and back.

Nov 1915: In due course our Division received embarkation orders and consequently we had a lot of inspections. The King, Lord Kitchener and Lord Derby were to inspect us, but the King had an accident falling off his horse in France and Lord Kitchener was ill, so only Lord Derby came in the end. However, the King sent his regrets and said that by the accounts he had received we were one of the best trained Divisions to be sent overseas and he felt sure we would acquit ourselves well on the battlefields of France and earn as good a name there as we had here.

We also did an attack for the Lord Mayor of Manchester, who wished us God speed. The Bishop of Manchester preached at church parade that Sunday, his text being, "Strive to enter in by the narrow door," and shook hands with every man.

Bathing at Grantham, June/July 1915. From a postcard sent by Albert's mother to his father: "Coming home on the 10 past 8 from Grantham. Tom is coming with the soldiers on the 12.45. Albert is on this PC. I have put a dot on him."

The next fortnight was embarkation leave - half the Battalion the first week and the other half the second. There were 7 special trains from Salisbury to Manchester and I believe thousands met the trains coming in at London Road Station.

When my four days came, I didn't go on a troop train but went via London and Nottingham to see some friends, leaving London at 6.20 and Nottingham at two in the morning to arrive in Manchester at six. I had to leave Manchester at 10.30am on the Sunday to get back to Larkhill for seven that evening and my father came to the station to see me off. I remember him asking if there was anything I wanted and saying as he shook hands with me, "Do your duty. Do it well. Run no unnecessary risks," and off the train went.

The following week was spent in exercises and equipping us for active service. A kit for active service weighed about 100 lbs and apart from his rifle, bayonet and the clothes he wore, every soldier had to carry:

2 shirts
1 brush
2 pairs of pants
1 overcoat
1 vest
1 gas helmet in satchel
1 towel
1 oil sheet
4 pairs of socks
1 toothbrush
1 blanket
1 comb
iron rations
4 sandbags
150 rounds ammunition
1 hold-all

[The hold-all includes knife, fork, spoon, shaving brush, soap, razor and housewife for mending and sewing clothes.]

We handed in all our other clothing, including the blue uniform which the Manchester people had bought us [they subscribed £26,701.9.9d], and we were only allowed to carry the things on the list given to us. Early in the week several of us were ordered to pack our kit and be ready to move at one hour's notice as we were supposed to be an advance party. But no orders came and on the Saturday everyone was told to pack up.

7 Nov 1915: About 7.00am we paraded fully equipped for Active Service and marched to Amesbury, where we entrained. We didn't know where we were going but landed at Southampton about ten in the morning and waited on the docks until 4.00pm, when we were marched on to the boat. We put our rifles in racks, each had a lifeboat given to us and on a dirty, wet, misty Sunday night set sail, not knowing our destination. About an hour out to sea we got the order "Lights Out" and sentries were posted on deck.

August 1915, from a postcard. Albert is on the ground on the right: "A photo of us resting on the march coming from Ancaster after trench digging. We have just fallen out here for 10 minutes. You see I am just having a smoke."

First weeks in France

When the 19th Manchesters arrived in France, the British Army was in a kind of uncomfortable stalemate. 1914 had seen the Germans sweep through Belgium, the battle of Mons and the historic stand at Le Cateau (August), fighting on the Marne and the Aisne (September) and the transfer of the small, professional BEF northwards in preparation for the First Battle of Ypres towards the end of the year. The Ypres front was to keep them occupied for most of the following twelve months.

As Territorial Divisions became available in 1915, they were sent far afield to replace Regulars serving in India, Sudan and elsewhere, but even when these troops arrived in France, the regular army remained small. The long-drawn-out siege in the Dardanelles was also a drain on manpower until Gallipoli was finally evacuated in December. Initial success at Loos in September had turned into failure because the reserves, kept miles to the rear by a cautious Commander-in-Chief, were not available in time and feelings at home were running high. Edith Cavell had been executed on 12th October, there had been a Zeppelin raid on London the following day and Lord Derby's recruiting scheme was in full swing by the end of the month. Reinforcements in France were desperately needed if the war of attrition in the trenches was to be brought to an end.

But changes were on the way. Following the criticism after Loos, Sir John French resigned as Commander-in-Chief and was replaced by General Sir Douglas Haig in December. Early that month an Allied conference at Chantilly agreed to launch a simultaneous offensive on the Russian, Italian and French/Belgian fronts in the spring. This was eventually postponed until July, largely to give time for the armies to be organised; as one writer put it, "The British armies in the field for the first half of 1916 were one great training school." Much of this "training" was in the line, however, especially after the German attack on Verdun in February, when the British took over the French front at Arras to release French troops.

A new Fourth Army was formed under General Rawlinson to defend the trenches north of the River Somme and part of this Army was Sir Walter Congreve's XIII Corps, which included the 30th Division, with the 19th Manchesters in its 21st Brigade (they had been transferred from the 90th Brigade soon after their arrival in France.) In his first dispatch as Commander-in-Chief, dated 29th May 1916, Sir Douglas Haig summed up the situation: "A steady and continuous fight has gone on, day and night, above ground and below it. The comparative monotony of this struggle has been relieved at short intervals by sharp local actions, some of which, although individually almost insignificant in a war on such an immense scale, would have been thought worthy of a separate dispatch under different conditions."

On the March

8 Nov 1915: About 1.00am we saw the lights of a harbour which we found out later was Le Havre. We were kept on

Men of the BEF resting in a French town, 1914

board until eight in the morning and then marched off to a rest camp outside the town. Here I was made battalion room orderly, so did not get much rest. At 9.00 that night we were ordered to parade and marched to Le Havre station, where we were put in cattle trucks.

9 Nov 1915: The train left about three o'clock on Tuesday morning. We passed through Rouen and about 10.00am stopped at a small station, where we were given biscuits and bully beef for our breakfast and dinner. This was our first taste of iron rations and I could not manage the biscuits! Anyway, on and on we travelled to a place called Pont Remy not far from Amiens. Here we detrained and set off on a march I shall never forget.

After being stuffed in a cattle truck so long with very little sleep, I was tired, hungry and thirsty to begin with. We marched on to a place called St Riquier with men falling out on the way dead beat. Here we halted for an hour - it would be about 9.00pm by this time - and were told we could go and buy food if we could get any. Well, picture a small French village with troops already billeted in it and a thousand hungry fellows let loose! Someone had to go short. I managed to get a sandwich and a drink, but during this hour it began to rain. We fell in and marched off but the men were dead beat and after a while transport was wired for and we were ordered to put our valises on the transport. This helped a great deal but the conditions were still so miserable, we were dead tired. We marched on in the darkness through open country, wet through, along roads swimming with water. Water trickled down our bodies and our feet were sodden, but still the order came, "Keep going," and on we marched through the next village and the next.

Beaumetz

10 Nov 1915: It was 2.00am on Wednesday morning when we arrived at our destination, a small village called Beaumetz, and here 120 of us were billeted in a barn with a roof like a pepper box top. I had gone through a hole full of water in the dark and was soaked to the waist, but I was so dog tired I lay down just as I was with my equipment still on and fell fast asleep. However, I wakened about 4.00am trembling with cold and could not get to sleep again. I had brought a box of Woodbines to France with me but when I opened my pack next morning everything was wet through; worst of all, my cigs were all spoilt and crushed and I had to throw them away.

When a new Division arrives in France it is rationed for a few days with another and the rations vary a lot. You notice the shortage of bread more than anything: with one 2lb loaf between 6 to 12 men there is sometimes not more than one piece per man for 24 hours. The difference is made up with biscuits. The other rations were jam, cheese, and stew for dinner (at this time simply bully beef stewed) and a drink of tea for breakfast.

This was my first day in France and my feet had not been dry since I landed. My stockings were wet through in my pack and with the constant rain there was nowhere to dry them, but it would have been no use if they had been dry. My boots were saturated and the roads were so bad your feet would have been wet again in an hour's time.

11 Nov 1915: The next day we turned out and drilled on a ploughed field under our Company Commander. It was very tiring, the ground being so wet it stuck to your boots and in the afternoon it began to snow. Our Captain cancelled the afternoon parade owing to the weather, but the Colonel ordered us out and made us do

Newly-arrived troops at a coffee stall in Le Havre, 1915

an hour's drill on the field in the storm, then formed us up and threatened what he would do if he had any more of this nonsense.

We were glad when we were marched back to the barn for tea - jam, cheese and biscuits. Another fellow and I set out to the village to try to buy some bread. I was refused at two or three houses but at last a French woman sold me half a loaf and the other fellow got a loaf, so off back to the billet we went and our section had a good feed.

12 Nov 1915: Another day of hard work at drill and very little food. I was getting desperate for a smoke, but we could send letters now [this had so far been forbidden] and we went into a café from where I wrote home to my parents, asking them to send me a parcel and plenty of Woodbines as I was hungry and had not had a smoke for days. We ordered bottles of wine and returning to the billet quite merry, lay on the straw with our blankets over us and went to sleep.

14 Nov 1915: On the Sunday morning it was very cold and I went to a café early and asked for a glass of coffee, for which the usual charge was a penny. The coffee wasn't ready and while I was waiting, the French woman took hold of a dirty towel, dipped it into the coffee pan, rubbed some soap on it and wiped her face. I suppose this was her wash, but it was my drink of coffee! I said I would not wait, asked for a packet of biscuits and went back to the billet to hold out until tea came up at breakfast time.

Monday was pretty much the same and on Tuesday the orders came to move.

17 Nov 1915: Starting off about 8.00am next morning, we marched through Canaples to a place called Flesselles, a distance of about fifteen miles. Raining again! Here we stayed the night.

Coisy

18 Nov 1915: Off again at 7.30 and arrived at a village called Coisy about five miles from Amiens. Here we were billeted in a barn where the rats used to run over us at nights and we each had to take a turn at doing one hour's billet sentry duty - this was in case of unusual occurrences such as fire or gas. You would probably be nicely warm and asleep when you would be wakened and have to turn out in the cold for your hour on.

19 Nov 1915: The first morning there we had to break the ice to get water to have a wash and shave, and bread was still very hard to get, but that afternoon I was roaming about the village and discovered a bakehouse. In I went and bought three loaves. All the fellows who saw me coming down the street asked where I had got them from and I told them. That baker very soon had no bread! I think by this time I would have given anything for a Woodbine, my favourite cigarette (I smoke no others).

We stayed in that village about ten days, doing all kinds of

The movements of the 19th Manchesters from arrival at Pont Remy in November 1915 to the return to Bray at the end of June 1916 before the Somme battle

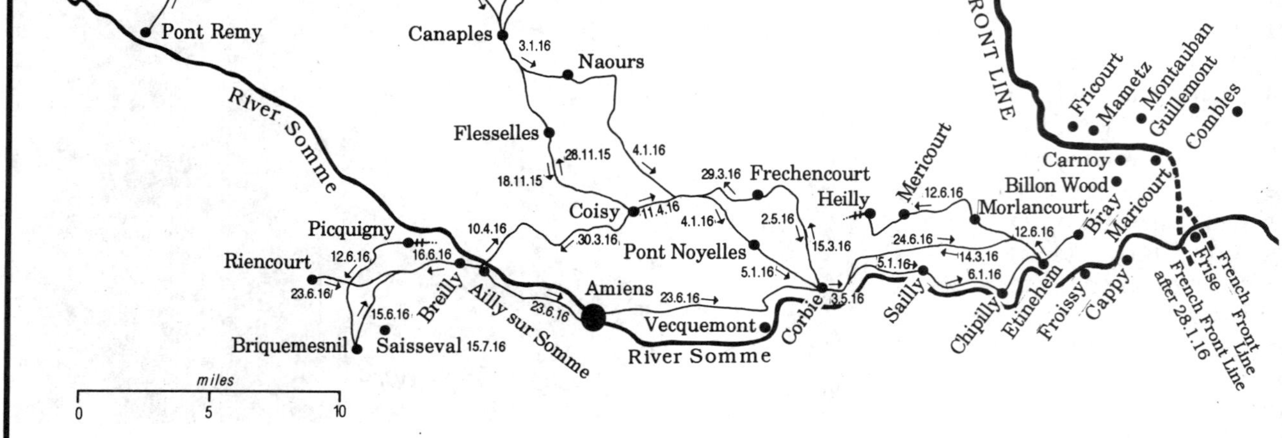

drills. One day we paraded at 2.00pm and were informed that we had to pay compensation for damage done to the barn at Beaumetz. Our Platoon's share was 40 francs. I myself would not have paid that for the whole village, but anyway 1 franc was stopped out of our next pay.

At night we used to visit the café, drinking and gambling, mainly at Crown and Anchor. The last Saturday night there about 6 of us were pretty well full with wine and having some bad luck. I think we backed the Heart to win ten times and it did not turn up. At last our Corporal, who had been gambling with us, said, "I've only one franc left and I'm saving that for tomorrow to get a drink."

I only had two francs and was going to go back to the billet with him, but just then one of my pals put his last ten shilling note on the Heart. I told the Corporal, "If he can put his last ten shillings on, I can throw my last two francs," and the Corporal gave me his money, saying, "Well, put this on with yours." We lost again and out we all came, broke. I had one halfpenny left but was quite happy.

I might mention here that the reason we went into the café drinking and gambling was that it was not pleasant sitting in a dirty old barn. We were nearly always wet through, our feet never dry, and we were hungry; the wine used to make us forget.

When we arrived back at the billet there was a letter and a parcel from home, nearly all of us getting one. Of course, the parcels received the first attention and I think they all got a good caning - and the Woodbines were there! Now I was happy. I had heard from home, had a good feed and plenty of Woodbines to smoke.

Canaples

28 Nov 1915: But we were moving again on the Sunday morning. Our packs were heavy but we made sure the remainder of those parcels was carried! We marched out of Coisy to a village called Canaples, where we were billeted in a kind of loft with pigs underneath. I remember an old French woman coming up one night; she wakened us all up, shouting and asking for help with a cow she owned. A few of us obliged.

We stayed in this village about ten days and had an easier time here, simply doing fatigues or a couple of hours' drill per day. Most of the time we paraded about 7.00am, marched to a wood about 6 miles away and spent the day felling trees and sawing them up, arriving back for tea about 4.30. But my feet had still not been dry for one day since I had arrived in France.

On Sunday we had to dig trenches. I was watching one of our aeroplanes and a German fighting overhead one day, when a nose cap from a shell fell and buried itself in the ground about a yard from where I was digging. It had probably been fired at one or other of the 'planes, but it was near enough to me not to be nice!

On and On

7 [8] Dec 1915: On the Tuesday we marched from Canaples to a

The main square of shell-torn Arras

place called Halloy [east of Doullens], a distance of about 20 miles. I know after the first ten miles this kind of life was beginning to tell, for I could not lift my equipment up to swing it on my back. We halted ten minutes in every hour, and I used to have to lie down on my back, put my arms through the straps, roll on to my stomach, on to my knees and up. I think it was on this march that one man, completely done up, lost his temper, threw the pack down and said, "There's the ****ing pack. Let the ****ing Transport take it!" and refused to carry it. Going up a very steep hill about two miles from our destination the Battalion was almost crawling along, absolutely tired out.

The Colonel riding at the side said, "Come on, lads, keep on keeping on," and pointing to a tower, he said, "That is where you are going." We arrived there about 5.00pm, dead tired.

8 [9] Dec 1915: The next morning we paraded at 8.00am and marched off again, but had not got many miles when it started raining and the muddy roads and the march of the day before began to take their toll. That morning, there being a shortage of rations, our Section was given bully and biscuits. I never could eat the biscuits so had a drink of tea only before we set off. Of course, after about 7 miles I was absolutely beat! I kept saying I would fall out but somehow still kept sticking it. Several of my mates had fallen out already, two collapsing completely and having to be put in the ambulance.

I think we had covered about 15 miles when we arrived at Berles au Bois, a village 600 yards from the firing line on the left of Monchy [au Bois], south-west of Arras. The first food I had that day was my tea, about 4.00pm.

Christmas and New Year

First Time in the Trenches

11 Dec 1915: The Germans shelled us in this village and a day or two later we went up to the front line. The Germans were only 400 yards away but the first day was very quiet and at six at night I was told off for listening post. It had been raining for several days and the trenches were knee deep in mud. A Sergeant took me out into No Man's Land along with another chap and picked out a suitable spot for me to lie down, then found one for the other chap not so far away. The duty was one hour on and two off and when that hour of lying in the mud was up, I was frozen nearly. The next hour I could go in the dugout and the one after that stand in the trench - what is called "standing by". At 9.00pm it was my turn out again. You had to get over the top and through the wire into No Man's Land to relieve. I did that hour, but could hardly stand the cold and was on again at twelve midnight. This was my worst hour of all. It rained, hailed and blew a proper gale.

To give an idea of how cold it was, I had my canvas mess tin cover on my back and when I was relieved it was frozen quite stiff. I could hardly feel my hands and legs and could not

A mud-filled trench

keep a limb still, I was so cold, but I had to do another hour and that was my first night in No Man's Land.

Another night I was out wiring, which was not half so bad as the weather was much better. We had a few casualties, but this part of the line was very quiet at that time. For instance, there was a canteen and a piano which we played. You could hear the singing in the fire trench, but it seemed to be a case of, "If you don't shell our billet, we won't shell yours."

On the Move Again

About the middle of December we received orders to move again, none of us at all sorry as in those trenches several of our men got stuck in the mud up to their waist, could not move and had to be dug out.

[17 Dec] 1915: We marched to a place called La Herlière, a small village half way between Arras and Doullens which was about 5 miles behind the fighting line. Here we did fatigues most of the time. On one guard duty from midnight to 2.00am it had been snowing very heavily and I was watching the lights go up from the trenches, when I was told to keep a sharp lookout as there was a spy about, dressed in a British officer's uniform. I never saw a soul! While in this village I received several Christmas parcels and cigarettes, so had a good time.

24 Dec 1915: On Christmas Eve we had orders to move again and marched off, covering about 12 miles and reaching Halloy about 6.00pm. Just before starting this march I had a new pair of boots which rubbed my heel and when I came to pull my boot off my stocking was saturated in blood. I showed the hole in my heel to the Officer at foot inspection and he ordered me to the Doctor to get it bandaged. This I did and then about six of us went off to a café. It was Christmas Eve and we were going to have a drink together.

Making the Most of It

Well, we mixed one wine with another and came rolling back to the billet, all of us as full up as we could be. Once inside the billet we started larking about, throwing things at one another. I know next morning I found one of my boots outside the barn and did not find my hat until ten minutes before parade time. Of course, I was not the only one - some lads lost half their things in the straw and never saw them again.

25 Dec 1915: We marched out of Halloy on Christmas morning through Doullens, this being the first place I had seen in France worth calling a place; the others were nothing else but old barns. We covered about 15 miles to Boisbergues. It snowed all the time we were marching and we had bully beef stew for dinner about 3.00pm. I put my mess tin down with a drop of it in and one of the fellows accidentally kicked it over. That was my Christmas dinner and a piece of bread and jam was my tea!

26 Dec 1915: Next day I was warned for fatigues and when I came in at dinner time I was told there was a parcel and a letter for me. Of course, as usual with all soldiers' parcels at first, it was from home. My mother had sent a chicken ready cooked and a small Christmas pudding. This, I can tell you got a right good caning. I made up for Christmas dinner!

In this village, apart from doing all kinds of fatigues, we were taught bombing and wiring drill. We were put through a gas chamber to test our helmets and shown in lectures how to put them on quickly.

28 Dec 1915: We had lectures on the new trenches we were

A wiring party

going to take over and were told it was a very quiet front generally. It was the Breslau Poles who were in the German trenches, men who did not want to fight.

One night a few of us went into a café where a good many French soldiers were sitting, drinking, gambling and arguing. They tried to get us to sing "Tipperary". We said we would sing it if they would pay for drinks all round, but no! "No money," they said, and they got no "Tipperary".

We came out well away but we did not care - it was a lot better than sitting in a miserable dirty barn all night. As we were going down the road we were stopped by our Officer, but all he said was, "Been having a night out, boys? Well, get in and to bed and be quiet."

It was after this I thought I would mend my ways, I was so ill, but it was useless to say I would not drink or I would have no pals and nowhere to go. You could not go for a walk, not being allowed out of the village without a pass, and these were only granted for special reasons.

On New Year's Eve we went to the midnight service and early on Monday morning we were ordered to pack up and stand to, our breakfast going west that morning. But it was only a trial to see if we could do it in the hour, as every Battalion is supposed to be able to move at an hour's notice.

Keeping On

3 Jan 1916: About 10.00am we marched off from Boisbergues, the start of a four days' march. My heel was not better and after a few hours I began to limp very badly. Going through Canaples, our Officer must have noticed me limping and came up and asked what was the matter. I told him it was my heel and he said I could fall out if I wished. I answered no. "You have never fell out yet, Andy, have you?" he said. "Well, we have only about five miles to go. If you can stick it, go to the doctor when we get there and tell him I have sent you." I managed to stick it, but was in pain all the time and was glad to get it bandaged by the doctor. We marched 14 miles that day to a place called Naours.

The next morning we were off again and marched to a place called Pont Noyelles, stayed there the night and off again the next day, marching to a place called Sailly le Sec. We were all feeling about done by this time, but next day off again.

6 Jan 1916: This was our trying day. We could not start before three in the afternoon as after a few miles we were under observation from the German lines. We marched out of Sailly on the low road, passing through Bray sur Somme about 10.00pm.

We went stumbling along that Bray road in the dark - you could not see a thing in front of you - over the ankles in mud and water and every now and then going into a shell hole and getting soaked to the waist. It was blowing and raining like fury and to crown all the Germans began to shell us. This was where I said I would not care if a Jack Johnson hit me full in the chest!

British artillery and German prisoners passing through Sailly le Sec

Round About Bray

Drawing Rations

Anyway, after a great struggle we arrived at Billon Wood about midnight, still tripping over twigs and falling in shell holes. Here we were about one mile from the firing line and we were put in canvas tents, but we had not been in the tent many minutes when we were called out again to go and draw rations. The transport used to bring them up to about half a mile from the wood and we had to go out of the wood by a sunken road which was nearly all shell holes. We picked up our loads and started off back to the wood down this sunken road.

I had four sandbags, two on each shoulder, and one of my mates had a large piece of beef to carry. We had only gone about 100 yards when I heard such a splash in front of me! It was my mate. He had fallen into a shell hole and gone full length in the mud, and the beef with him. He started swearing for all he was worth. I laughed and he cursed me too! Anyway, he picked up his beef but had not gone very far before he was full length again. He was up again and off, still swearing, when I heard a shout in front of us: "Keep clear!" It was a water cart. They had nearly run over my mate in the dark and he'd had to drop the beef in the mud and scramble up the side of the sunken road. Well, he stood and cursed that transport driver for what seemed like five minutes!

Eventually I said, "Come on, let's get on. I will take the lead." But I hadn't gone far before I stepped out and the ground was not there. Into a deep shell hole full of water I went, then I began to let steam off! My mate went down two or three times after this, the beef being difficult to get along with, and when we arrived back in the wood I heard him say to someone in the dark, "I don't ****ing care what they do to me, I am not going to wrestle any more ****ing cows up that road in the ****ing dark any more!"

In and Out of the Line

8 Jan 1916: On Saturday night about 5.00pm we went by communication trenches up to the firing line in 52 trench. I was on fatigues - cleaning the trench, carrying rations, any kind of jobs - the first two days and the next two on sentry. This really means keeping a sharp lookout for anything unusual, but you trust to your ears mostly by night and use your nose for gas. Of course, by day you can usually see gas coming, depending on the wind. By day you do 2 hours on and 4 off and by night one on and two off, but you are not allowed to leave the bay where you are on duty during your time off. The sentry has with him a first relief, who must not sleep, and a second relief, who may - but not much sleep does he get; it is too cold and wet.

The routine in the trenches is supposed to be as follows. Every man stands to at dusk and dawn for one hour and after dawn you receive your rum ration, then you clean your rifle for inspection about 8.00am. Breakfast may be boiled bacon and tea, dinner stew, and tea bread and butter or jam, with a cup of tea at midnight.

There are six after dusk on each sentry post and after dawn only three. The others are put on fatigues, pumping water out of the trench, for example. All cartridge cases are collected and put into a sandbag. By each sentry there is a gas gong which he rings if there is any gas about. There is a sentry on each dugout door, ready to warn the men who may be asleep if anything unusual happens. One of our fellows was charged with being asleep on this duty: the Officer said he was, he said he was not. Anyway, he got 15 years for it, which was later reduced to 7.

Rations

12 Jan 1916: Well, the first four days passed all right and we were relieved by the 2nd Wiltshire Regiment [19th King's Liverpool Regiment]. I should mention here that we had been put in the 21st Brigade, which consisted of a Battalion of Liverpools, the 2nd Yorks, 2nd Wilts and our Battalion, the 19th Manchesters. The relief was at midnight and we went back about a mile to Billon Wood. We were what they called supports to the firing line.

Here we spent another four days going up to the fire trench doing mining fatigues. As they dug, the miners filled sandbags with the earth which the Infantry carried out - and it was very hard work. When you have done eight hours of this, you are lucky if you get eight hours off, and if you do it is rifle inspection, gas helmet inspection, equipment inspection - anything but five minutes to call your own. Rations had to be brought up at ten o'clock every night - I have already described what that was like!

16 Jan 1916: After four days of this we went back into the fire trench and here did another four days' sentry and fatigues, going down to Carnoy, a small village just beyond the fire trench.

The only bright part was for about half an hour after the rum had been issued following stand to at dawn. This we were glad to get as we were nearly always wet through and trembling with cold; the rum warmed us. I know one of these nights I lay on the firestep in the mud while I was third relief, which meant an hour's sleep. When they wakened me to do my hour's sentry, I was wet through - I had slept through a thunderstorm.

I was on sentry with five of my mates and the wind was bitterly cold that night so we pulled the flaps of our soft caps over our ears, not knowing it was wrong. Two of my mates, Robinson and Baillie, were on duty at the time the C/O came round - he used to visit us every night between eleven and one. He asked them what they were doing with their hats like that and how did they ****ing well expect to hear anything, and took their names. We had a few casualties during this time.

20 Jan 1916: At the end of this four days we marched to Bray, a village about 6 miles from the fire trench. It's when soldiers come out at midnight that the effects of winter in the trenches are seen. They are not as you see a Battalion marching in England, it being impossible to keep them together. They come staggering along, perhaps 20, then about 6, then 2, splashing in the mud, covered in the stuff and absolutely beat, with not an ounce of strength left in them. I myself had not had a wash or shave for 16 days. You never see the colour of your hands for dry clay and everything you touch gets covered with mud, the difficulty being to keep your rifle in working order.

We might not get to Bray until 2.00am, but at 6.00am so many were warned for mining fatigues, which meant going back to the trenches and working for six hours or more. If it wasn't that, it was road cleaning, RE fatigues or building dugouts. If you escaped all this, you had to turn out by 12 mid-day clean and shaved, with your boots washed, clothes scraped and brushed and rifle and bayonet cleaned. Four days of this was worse than being in the firing line except that we had a little more sleep!

[23 Jan] 1916: My two mates Baillie and Robinson were sent for from a fatigue party to report to Battalion HQ at Bronfay Farm, 2 miles behind the fire trench. This was to be

Bray in 1918

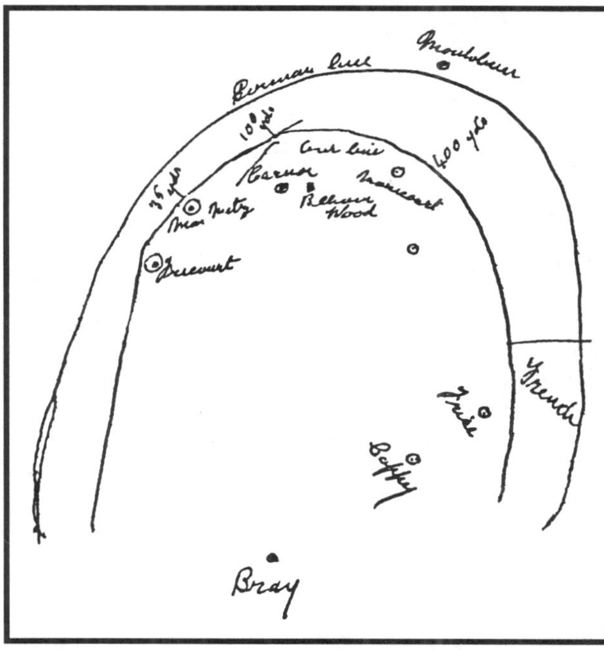

Albert's sketch map of the front line near Carnoy before the French lost Frise and Cappy

tried for having the flaps of their caps down. While they stood waiting a shell came, killing Baillie instantly. Robinson, his back and head badly damaged, died four hours later at the dressing station. This was another two pals gone.

24 Jan 1916: After our four days in Bray, back again to the firing line.

28 Jan 1916: The fourth day, I believe, being the Kaiser's birthday, all was quiet during the day and we had had orders to pack up after tea. Our sentry group, all pals, had just set our tea out on the firestep, when bang! Fritz dropped one quite close and sent the parapet over our tea. No tea that night for us!

A German Attack

This was the starting of a strafe, Fritz sending shrapnel, high explosive rifle grenades and "sausages", as we used to call them, or canisters. One of these, dropping quite close to our bay, blew sandbags in the air and a sentry in our group got one full in the back. He was carried away on a stretcher. Our two Platoon Sergeants were in their dugout and that was blown in. We had to dig them out and one of them was taken away on a stretcher too.

About 8.00pm we were informed that we could not be relieved that night. The German shellfire was too heavy to risk sending troops or transport up the road.

That did it! About 9.00pm we were all ordered to stand to and the alarm was given for gas. The Germans were going to attack. Well, they bombed us and the Liverpools but we repulsed them - their main attack was really on the French. Few of that German bombing party got back. One of their officers, a fine fellow, was going to give himself up when a York spotted him.

"Look at this ****er!" he said. "He thinks he's going to Blighty. Well, I cannot go, so he cannot," and let him have a bomb all to himself, which sent him west.

However, the French on our right lost several lines of trenches, including the village of Frise and the Germans got into Cappy, a place two-and-a-half miles from Bray. We were in a horse shoe about 6 miles from Bray and the German effort was to try and close the horse shoe and so capture a few thousand men in the ring. Fortunately the French counter-attacked and retook some of the lost ground. They did not get Frise back but at least it made our position at the top of the horse shoe more secure.

Australians with German prisoners in Cappy in 1918

Casualties

29 Jan 1916: The strafe continued all next day and that night we were relieved. After five days of it we had all had enough, and I had lost a few of my mates killed and wounded. When you turned round and looked, after coming out of the trenches, what with killed, wounded and sick, we were getting less. The weather and the strain alone had cracked quite a few up.

We did another four days in Bray. The band used to play in the square from two to three in the afternoon and of course all the soldiers used to go to listen. They had just cleared away one afternoon when the Germans dropped a shell right into the middle of the square, killing and wounding some French women. I believe the Germans shelled Bray about three o'clock every day for a few weeks after this. Of course, everyone went to the cellars while this was on.

The next four days it snowed nearly every day and after we had done our four, the General ordered two days only in the fire trench while it was cold. This meant us having only two days in support before returning to the fire trench, and I remember doing another four days there in the snow.

13 Feb 1916: Coming down to Bray after that four days, still one or two less in our Platoon which would be about 26 strong by then, one of our Corporals and two men lay on the side of the road and fell fast asleep. Our Colonel spotted them later on (he was the last to leave the trenches, of course), wakened them up and asked what they were doing there. They told him. "Oh," he said, "you are my lads, are you? Well, come along with me. Keep on keeping on. I know you're ****ed up and fed up, but get to Bray to your billet and have a proper sleep."

19th Manchesters

Casualties January - March 1916

b = birthplace as listed in *Soldiers Died in the Great War*

KIA = Killed in Action. DoW = Died of Wounds

12599 Pte Matthew White		KIA 19 Jan
11735 Pte William Baillie	b Openshaw	DoW 23 Jan
12525 Pte Albert Robinson	b and lived Northwich	DoW 23 Jan
11715 Pte Harry Woodfin	b and lived Swinton	Died 27 Jan
12473 Pte William E Thirlwell	b Hulme	DoW 28 Jan
12103 Sgt John Heywood	b Manchester, lived Middleton	DoW 29 Jan
11752 Pte Albert Brandreth	b Broughton	DoW 3 Feb
12410 Pte Stephen Massey	b Miles Platting	KIA 4 Feb
11790 Pte Harold Dickinson	b Prestwich	DoW 5 Feb
12044 Pte Frederick R Cooke	b Openshaw	KIA 6 Feb
12056 Cpl George A Crowe	b Cheetham	KIA 6 Feb
12113 Pte George William Hope	b Little Drayton, Salop	KIA 6 Feb
12934 Pte Thomas Wilkinson	b Gorton	DoW 6 Feb
12659 Pte Harry Hodkinson	b Bradford, Manchester	DoW 11 Feb
11897 Pte Samuel Newman	b Chorlton on Medlock	DoW 11 Feb
12114 Pte Philip Frederick Hover	b Patricroft	KIA 12 Feb
12248 Pte Jose Woolley	b Butterton, Staffs, lived Sandbach	KIA 12 Feb
12043 L/Cpl Samuel Condliffe	b Sandbach, lived Stockport	KIA 13 Feb
12834 Pte Tom Wilson	b and lived Bury	KIA 13 Feb
12033 Sgt Stanley Carter	b Manchester	DoW 25 Feb
12421 Pte Arthur Garnett Penn	b West Bromwich, lived Bootle	KIA 26 Feb
12863 Pte Henry Grundy	b Atherton	KIA 2 Mar

14 Feb 1916: The next day one of my pals that had been on sentry with me in the trenches was to be tried. On my hour sentry the Corporal had relieved me late each time, and the last time he was ten minutes overdue, so he got told off - my mate Travis was next up, deliberately relieved him late and told him about it. The Corporal said something back to him and got hit on the nose for saying it!

The C/O tried Travis and gave him 7 days Number One field punishment, which means being kept in the Guard Room, fed on bully and biscuits and "crucified", as we called it, to a cart wheel for so many hours a day. But the C/O let all prisoners off their punishment this time in Bray, saying we were being punished enough.

During this time my heel hurt me but I took no notice, until one night in the trenches I could not put my foot to the ground and I was taken on a stretcher to hospital. Half way there we were in the middle of this crossroads when the Germans suddenly started shelling it and the stretcher bearers dropped me and dived for cover. I thought, "I'm going to have more than a ****ing bad foot here!" However, they came back and took me safely to Chipilly Hospital, where I stayed six days while they tried to get the poison out of my foot. As soon as it was clear, I was discharged and went back to my Battalion, which was in Billon Wood.

By this time we were all walking away with lice, it being useless to try and keep clean. If you had a bath and a change of clothes, you were as bad as ever 12 hours afterwards. We used to have what they called "delousing parades", which involved taking your things off and killing as many as you could. At times you could not sleep at night for them.

A Well Earned Rest

None Too Healthy

[7/8] Mar 1916: At the beginning of March our Division at last got orders to go back for a rest. We were relieved from Billon Wood by the Royal Fusiliers about 10.00pm and we marched to Etinehem Wood, about four miles beyond Bray, where we were accommodated in tents. We spent all the next day cleaning up, scraping mud off clothes and so on, then we were inspected.

Six of the 19th Manchesters casualties for January and February 1916. Left to right: Sgt John Heywood, aged 22, lived at Westbourne, Sunny Brow Road, Middleton, and worked for the Lancashire & Yorkshire Bank in Oldham. Pte Stephen Massey, aged 25, lived in Laverton Place, Churnet Street, Miles Platting.

Pte Frederick Reginald Cooke lived in Rosina Street, Higher Openshaw, and worked for Hickson, Lloyd & King (merchants) of Manchester. Cpl George Alexander Crowe, aged 22, lived in Marshall Place, Cheetham Hill, and worked for C & W Walmsley (cotton manufacturers), Manchester. Pte Thomas Wilkinson, aged 18, lived in Gorton Road, Reddish, and worked at the Broadstone Mills, Reddish. Pte Philip Frederick Hover lived in Charlton Avenue, Patricroft.

We were here about a week and our work was cleaning out a communication trench named Maricourt Avenue. This meant marching about 8 miles to do three hours work and 8 miles back, Maricourt Avenue being a trench leading up to the fire trench. This went on for four days and there were only about ten of our original Platoon left by this time.

[12] Mar 1916: On the fourth day going to this fatigue I was beat, absolutely done up and feeling ill. Gradually I dropped back until I was at the end of the fatigue party and it was taking me all my time to keep going. Our Captain was riding behind and said to me, "What's this, Andy? You are not falling out, are you?" I said I could not go any further; I was done. "Come on," he said. "Show these new ones what the old ones can do," but I said I had done my best and could not go on.

We were going through Bray at this time, so he said, "Sit down and have a rest and then try and follow on." I waited a little time but was no better, so I got on a transport which carried me half way back towards Etinehem Wood and then managed to walk the rest of the way. As soon as I got back I went to the doctor, who told me to go and lie down and excused me all duties. I was suffering from exhaustion and cold, but

Corbie, "the first decent place we had seen..."

was soon fit again after a couple of days doing easy work.

[14] Mar 1916: We left Etinehem Wood for a place called Corbie. This was the first decent place we had seen, the first sign of any life at all. We arrived about 2.00pm and after several inspections three of us went out together. We had always said in the trenches that if ever we got our knees under a table again, we would have a good feed, so as soon as we spotted a cafe in we went.

The French girl there said they had only vanillas and cream buns, so we had a pile of these and tea, arriving back at the billet about 8.30pm. We were in the top room of the house sleeping on the floor, and we hadn't been in bed long when one of the lads I had been out with said he felt ill. "I'm not at my best," I said, and about ten minutes later jumped out of my bed and was sick through the window. This set my mate off and the other one too and we carried on all night, I being the last to stop and settle down at four in the morning. It was fried bacon for breakfast but we didn't want any! We couldn't touch the stew for dinner either, so at tea time we went into a cafe and chanced two boiled eggs each and bread and butter. This soon put us right again.

[15] Mar 1916: The next day we were off again and marched to a place called Fréchencourt about 12 miles away. Here we stayed ten days or more, making a railway. Wet or fine, we worked from 7 until 4.30 digging, carrying, all kinds of things. It was here I spent my birthday (19th March). A parcel arrived from home with a chicken ready cooked wrapped in a small Union Jack, but I was ill that day and after the work went straight to bed.

A Happy Time

[29/30] Mar 1916: At the end of our time here we marched off again to a place called Coisy, where we had been once before, stayed there the night and then off again to a place called Breilly [west of Amiens], covering about 25 miles in the two days. It was here I spent my happiest time in France. It was a nice, small country village and we were billeted in a cowshed (which we had to clean out before we could sleep in it!) We used to drill as we did in England to sharpen us up, and go out doing route marches and attacks. With this exercise in nice weather, being out in the open all day and getting good food with parcels from home, I was as fit as a fiddle in a few days.

6 Apr 1916: We had drill all day until 6th April, when we had a half day holiday [Brigadier General C J Sackville West inspected the Battalion that day]. With two of my chums, I got a pass to visit Picquigny. We spent the time looking round the place and I bought a pendant for my sister and a brooch made like a French 75mm gun.

Then it was drill all day for a few days, but was enjoying it, the weather being grand. During our stay here we had two or three drafts which filled up the Battalion and in the evening we used to spend our time in the café. One night we were going there for fried chipped potatoes and eggs and one of these fellows said, "Order me some. I will be down in a few minutes." Of course we

Picquigny, where Albert spent his half day off in April 1916

ordered one for him, one of my mates paying for the lot. In comes this chap, picks up his coffee which was at the side of his plate and says, "How much is this?" We answered, "1d," meaning the coffee - the meal itself was 10d each. Coming out, the chap said, "That was a ****ing good feed for 1d. Who do I owe it to?" He was soon informed different!

Another time we had been buying eggs at a farm and he came up and asked what you said to get them. We told him, "Der Earfs" (deux oeufs) if he wanted two, but he turned to the French woman and said, "Der Turfs".

Of course she answered him, "Non compris", to which he said, "It's funny. The other ****er has got them." It provided us with a laugh and then we corrected him so he could get his eggs.

[10] Apr - 2 May 1916: On 11th April we marched to Coisy and the following day left Coisy, arriving back at Fréchencourt. We stayed here until May 2nd, working making the railway, which was nearly ready for use.

Back to Bray

Into the Line

2/3 May 1916: Marched to Corbie, about 15 miles, stayed there the night and left about 4.00pm the next day, arriving at Bray about 10.00pm. The reason we left so late was that after a few miles we were under observation from the German lines and we would be harder to see at night. I know I was picked to draw rations when we arrived and was waiting until two in the morning for them.

4 May 1916: I was up again at five, it being my turn to do orderly. After breakfast we marched to Billon Wood.

We were on fatigues here on what we called "Russian saps", that is a tunnel being dug from our trench to the Germans'; the distance between us in the sap we were working was about 400 yards. We only left about a foot of earth over our heads, and this was propped up every yard. The saps were being dug, I might mention, for the Somme battle, the idea being that after the Infantry had captured the front German trench, the Pioneers simply knocked the top in and it was a communication trench from our lines to theirs for men bringing food, water and ammunition up to the troops attacking.

8 May 1916: From Billon Wood we went into the fire trench in front of Carnoy and Mametz Wood, in behind the German lines. I had been in these trenches from Fricourt, which was nothing but mines, to Carnoy. We relieved at 9.00pm on May 8th. I was not a bomber but we had a good many new men with us and I was put with the bombers on a bombing post. I did not mind because I was with the old boys. We were told to keep a sharp lookout as it was a dangerous post, the Germans having broken through there two weeks before.

The first night was all right but very wet, the trenches being filled with water very quick. The sentry on duty has to challenge anyone coming down his own trench, and about

A supply train arriving at Fréchencourt in March 1917

midnight we could tell someone was coming by the splashing.

"Halt! Who are you?" said one of our sentry group.
"I don't know," was the reply. "A ****ing submarine or something," and he called out, "Anything doing, sentry?"
"No," was the reply. "All right. I am not coming any further," he said. "What a ****ing place this is!"

9 May 1916: The next night the sniping of Fritz on our post was very hot, being a lot too near at times to be comfortable, but my mate and I just let go every now and then to let them know we had not gone home. About 1.00am I had just got my rifle up to fire when Fritz put one right in our parapet. Burying itself in the earth, it sent some in my eyes, nearly blinding me. I had to get off the fire step, one of my pals relieving me until I got my eyes right. When I could see again I jumped up on the firestep in a bad temper and just as I got up, he fired once more.

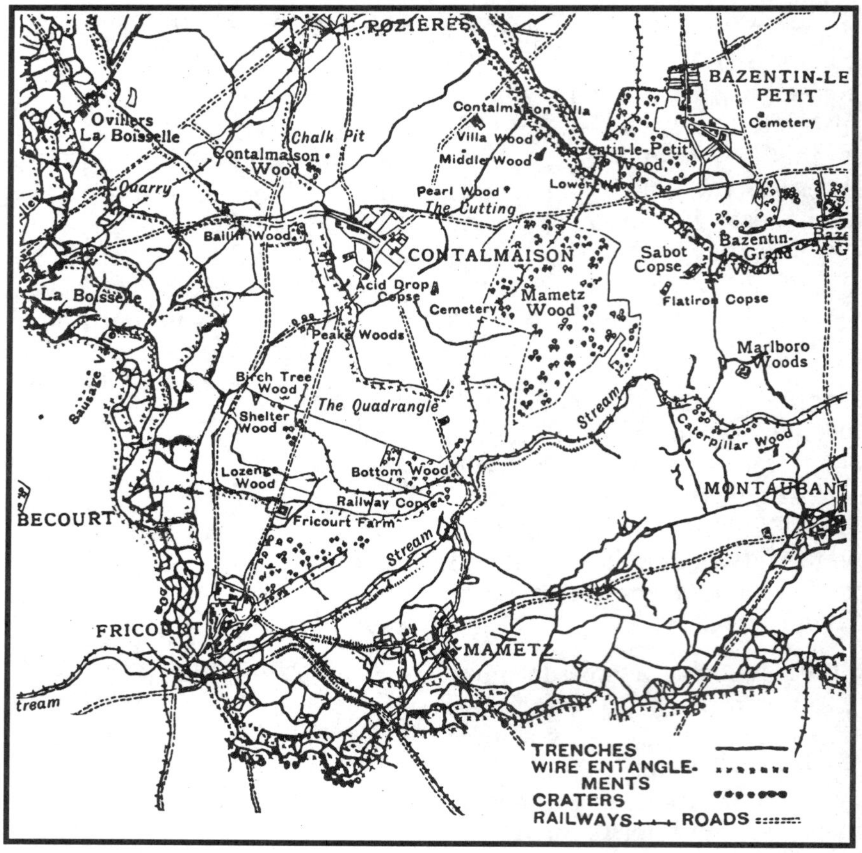

The German trench system between Fricourt and Montauban

My mate and I both spotted by the flash of his rifle where he was, so I said, "Should we have five rounds rapid at that spot, Herbert?"
"If you like," he said, and so we did.

Well, all was quiet after this for about ten minutes. My mate said, "We must have hit him or he has gone to sleep." I jumped on two sandbags nearby, exposing my body over the parapet, and thud! Something dropped right on the sandbag I was leaning against. We both dived and ducked down - of course, we would have been too late. When nothing happened, we felt about in the dark and I picked something up right under my nose. It was a rifle grenade. This is a large bomb on a rod, fired like a rocket and intended to drop into the trench. This was what had dropped on the sandbag right in front of me, but luckily it did not go off. If it had, I would have been in pieces! I had been near before, but this was too near!

Good News

We did a week in this time, coming out to Bray on Tuesday 16th about 2.00am.

17 May 1916: Early next morning I was warned for guard at a bridge over a canal called Froissy bridge, which meant all day scraping mud off my clothes, equipment and cleaning up generally. At five o'clock we mounted guard and had an easy 24 hours of it.

The next few days were occupied with RE fatigues, building dugouts. One morning we stood watching the Germans shell an RE dump we had just left, having called there for picks, shovels and so on.

27[20] May 1916: On the Saturday night I was just getting ready to go into the firing line again when they came and asked where I would like to spend my leave, as I was in the next lot to go. This was the first I had heard of leave and it brightened me up for the spell in the trenches.

Tom Andrews

We did six [four] days in front of Carnoy before being relieved by a battalion of another Division. During this six days I saw my brother Tom for the first time since I had left England; although we had only been half a mile away from one another most of the time, we had not met. In February he had walked fifteen miles to see me one day and missed me.

He had got leave to come this time because he was going into a bombing attack - he was a Headquarters bomber. I was under the German lines in one of these Russian saps when word was sent down he had come to see me. He had his tea with us and into the sap I and a few others went - these saps were very dangerous to work in just now as we were right under the German barbed wire.

The REs did not work after dusk because of German patrols who might hear them digging and we used to take it in turns at the top nearest the Germans, as we could hear them talking quite plainly at times. Fritz fired his machine gun once when I was at the top of the sap. It seemed right over my head and I walked down the sap a little way until he had finished - it was too near to be nice. There was such a bumping I expected the top coming in on me, and he and his machine gun with it.

According to the regimental history the Battalion went to Maricourt on 24 May; here they dug an advance trench with the 2nd Wilts and 2nd Beds and suffered many casualties. On 5 June they relieved the 2nd Wilts and took over the Maricourt defences, carrying out mining fatigues and working parties. The Battalion was so close to the front line at this point that the move to the fire trench itself probably appeared insignificant.

Hot and Wet

28 [24] May 1916: When we were relieved we went straight away and relieved another Battalion in front of Maricourt. The first few days were fine, the Poles being in, but we found the difference when the Prussians came; it was soon a hot shop. One of these fellows used to whistle all the English songs every night. Our machine gun would fire, but he only whistled again as soon as it had stopped to let us know it had not hit him.

It rained nearly every day about this time. I went down the communication trench (with full pack, of course) and coming back - it would be about 9.00pm - I sank into the mud up to the waist and had to wait there until someone came, and then they had to go and get tools to dig me out. I got free about 2.00am next morning, only to go a bit further up the trench and find two or three more men stuck as I had been.

By this time the Germans were letting us have it pretty hot they must have been beginning to see things! There were 400 yards between us here and one night a lot of the Bedfords and 2nd Yorks [Wilts] went out and dug a trench 200 yards from the Germans, our Battalion being the covering party. Only two men were wounded in this; we kept up the ordinary fire but sent our bullets in the air. This way, Fritz would not think anything was happening - you take it for granted that if the other side keep firing there are none of their men in between.

Behind the enemy lines. A German field kitchen

That was all right but next morning when the Germans saw the new trench they opened fire on us, knocking our trench down and killing and wounding our fellows. Our Battalion lost 50 in an hour's stand to. They kept it up all day, first one and then another being knocked over and then to cap it all it began to rain, the Germans still shelling us.

I was sent with some others for the midnight tea. We went at 10.30pm and arrived back at 5.00am next morning, and had only to go about three quarters of a mile for it. It comes up in a container about as large as a milk can and two of you carry this on a stretcher on your shoulders. We could not get along for the mud, and the stretchers and walking wounded coming down. I was standing near one of the Yorks Captains when he remarked they were making our boys pay dear for that trench. Anyway, after about three days they quietened down again.

Dark, Wet and Hungry

About 5 Jun 1916: A morning or two after I had had two rum issues and was firing at a sniper when the chap with me, whose nerves were not at the best, asked what I was firing at. I told him and he said, "Keep your head down or he will get you." Of course, with two good rum issues on an empty stomach I was three sheets in the wind and did not care whether the Germans were there or not. I said I would give the enemy three for every one. This chap said, "I'm going sick. I hope they throw them (bombs) at you as big as haversacks," and off he went.

Another night all was quiet until about 3.30am, when the Germans opened up with all their guns, shelling just on our right. I was on sentry and someone behind me asked if I could see anything. I turned round to reply and received a very smart, "Look to your front and answer." It was our Colonel!

I said no, I could not see anything.

"Is the Battalion stood to?"

"I think so," I replied.

Have you plenty of bombs and ammunition?"

"Yes, Sir."

"Do you want a light?" (meaning a Very light for me to see No Man's Land.)

I said no, glad to get rid of him. The attack was on the 90th Brigade, the Brigade my brother was in, but it was repulsed.

Another fatigue here was fencing round a cemetery for the Manchester lads who had fallen; it was in a valley called Death Valley. I came off this

Two of the 19th Manchesters casualties for May/June 1916. Pte Ernest Armsbey (left) lived in Cottenham Street, Chorlton on Medlock and worked for Richard Hudson & Sons of Newton Street, Manchester. Pte Robert Lamb Buckley, aged 21, lived in Sheldon Street, Clayton, and worked for the Great Northern Railway in Manchester

fatigue one day at 5.00pm and was warned for it again with ten others at 11.00pm. Just as we were entering the valley a thunderstorm commenced. It rained, blew, thundered and lightened and every now and then we would slip in the mud, measuring our length in it. To crown all, the Germans began to shell the valley about midnight. We could not see a hand in front of us and we were going to work in this on a cemetery of our own town's boys.

After a struggle we arrived at the RE dugout, only to find the officer in bed. He did not want us, especially on a night like that, and said, "It is a mistake you being sent." We did not swear - oh, no! - but at the same time were pleased we could get back out of it and after another struggle through the valley got back safely to the trench.

We heard Kitchener was drowned and about a naval battle [Jutland] where 18 of our ships had downed 3 of the Germans'. I won a franc on this, betting the Germans had lost more than us.

11 Jun 1916: On Whit Sunday morning my pal, who had asked for special leave because his father was dying, was sent

19th Manchesters

Casualties May - June 1916

b = birthplace as listed in *Soldiers Died in the Great War*

KIA = Killed in Action. DoW = Died of Wounds

12171 Pte George E Pattinson	b Northallerton	Died 4 May
12301 Pte Fred Coope	b Bury	KIA 11 May
12283 Pte Frank Blundell	b and lived Hindley	DoW 13 May
12105 Pte Stanley Hilton	b Prestwich	KIA 14 May
12205 Pte Ronald Hardy Slater	b Headingley, Leeds lived Bradford, Yorks	KIA 23 May
12683 Pte John Wilkinson	b Newcastle, Staffs lived Kidsgrove, Staffs	DoW 26 May
12419 Pte Cecil Owen	b Chorlton cum Hardy	KIA 31 May
12259 Pte Ernest Armsbey	b Chorlton-on-Medlock	KIA 31 May
12272 Pte Robert Lamb Buckley	b Clayton	Died 1 June
11863 L/Cpl Roy Jolley	b and lived Congleton	Died 1 June
26121 Pte Leonard Albert Jarvis	b Forest Gate, Essex lived Manor Park, Essex	DoW 6 June

for. We were working in one of the saps near the German lines knee deep in water and I remember calling after him, "If it is for leave, Dick, call at our house. Tell Ma I am all right and will soon be home to have a look at her." I went on working until 12 noon and then came out into the fire trench, hungry, thirsty and wet through, only to see one of my brother's Battalion, the 16th Manchesters, in the trench. He told me they were relieving us that night and I asked if my brother was all right and where I could find him. He directed me down one trench which ran under a building. Here I had to get on top and shout. Tom was in a dugout nearby and would hear me.

This I did and he answered, "Is that you, kid?"
I said, "Yes. Have you got your parcel from home?" I knew they had always received their parcels in the trenches; we did not and this was our third week in.

He said, "Yes. Are you hungry? Come here." We had a good feed, a little talk and a smoke, then I was off again; when I arrived up in our trench, my mate had gone on leave.

On the Move Again

Preparing for Battle

At midnight on Whit Sunday the 16th Manchesters, the Battalion my brother was in, relieved us and we marched from there to a place called Bois des Tailles [near Etinehem], a distance of about 12 miles. We had breakfast, then on again to Heilly and on the train to Picquigny, then marched another 10 miles to a place called Briquemesnil.

We arrived here about 10.00pm Whit Monday night, so we had spent Whit Monday travelling from midnight until ten o'clock the next night, and this was after three weeks in the trenches. None of us had a leg to stand on! [According to the regimental history, this relief was by the 17th Manchesters.]

Tues 13 Jun 1916: The next morning was spent in cleaning up and inspections. In the afternoon we marched out about 5 miles to a lot of open land. Here we found ourselves in amongst a lot of dummy trenches about a foot deep and it was here we were told we were for it. We were taken over to the dummy German trenches (our dummy trenches were just like the ones we had left) and it was all explained to us that there was going to be an attack. The 30th Division were in it and were going to attack this particular front, the 21st Brigade to lead the Division, with the 19th Manchesters and the Liverpools the first over. The 2nd Yorks were to support the Manchesters and the 2nd Wilts the Liverpools. We were to take the first three lines of trenches and Glatz Redoubt, a very strong position on the top of the crest in front of Montauban.

Us succeeding, the 90th Brigade would start coming over the ground we had won and carry on the attack to Montauban, through that village, then right turn. So we started to practise this, going over the ground time after time. We had one hour to do our share in, then we had tea and off out to see what there was in the village, returning about 8.30pm. It had been raining all day and what with practising the attack, going through long wet grass and lying down in the mud, we were just as dirty as ever.

A water supply point near Fricourt in July 1916

In Trouble

14 Jun 1916: Next day I was warned for guard with two of a draft that had just joined us. They were all right - their things were new and clean - but I had to be up at 5 o'clock cleaning, getting ready for guard at nine. The Orderly Officer who inspected us turned out to be a new one from England, one of those fellows that could see the star on his arm. He said, "Yes, they are very clean," but asked one of the draft, "When did you get your hair cut?"
"Four weeks since," was the reply.
"And yours?"
"About six weeks since," said the second man.
"And yours?" turning to me.
"Two days before we went into the trenches to do a guard there," I replied. We had only been out a couple of days!
"Crime all three," he said.

We did the guard, then went out with the others practising the attack. When we came back I waited until about six o'clock at night to see if I was sent for to be charged, but no, so off out I went with two of the old boys. We were coming back just nicely merry when I was told they had been looking for me all over - I was wanted to be charged! Anyway, we had our supper and off to bed.

[15/16 Jun] 1916: The next day we packed up and marched to Breilly, where we intended to stay, but the South Africans were there and would not move, there having been some mistake. We slept on the road that night and next morning we were marching back over the ground we had covered the day before. We had done about five miles and had ten to do when the whistle went for a halt of ten minutes. There was no room on the right hand side of the road, the side you fall out on in France, so some men of another Company and I fell out on the left side. I had hardly got my pack off when our Captain came and asked me, "Who gave you permission to fall out on the left hand side of the road?"
I said, "No-one."
As a matter of fact our Corporal had said, "Go on the other side, Andy," but I knew he had no authority to say it.
"Take his name, Sergeant."

We marched to a place called Riencourt, where we were to stay for a few days. I was eventually tried for the haircut that evening, along with the other two, the punishment being another guard, which we did the next day. But on the inspection it was the same Officer and he said one of the draft was dirty and a damn disgrace. (I agree he did not look smart!) The other one did not know or had forgotten how to fix bayonets, so he said, "Give them an hour's extra drill fixing bayonets every night." This meant me with them and he had found no fault with me!

As I recall, there were about three prisoners in the guard room doing Field Punishment Number One. I had a parcel brought me about tea time that had just come from home and after I had had my tea I handed the rest amongst them, I felt so

In the Somme valley, summer 1916

sorry for them. I was on sentry, so I just had to watch that the Police Sergeant did not catch them. I had arranged with them to bang the butt of my rifle on the stones outside if he was coming and they had a heap of straw ready to cover over the parcel. They just managed to get their feed when he came with the ropes to tie them to the wheel - I think that was the only serious watching I did on that guard!

18 Jun 1916: Next day after we had been out practising the attack, I had my tea and went off out again, returning about 8 o'clock to the billet. They had been looking for me to do this hour's fixing and unfixing bayonets, but I was missing again! Anyway, our Captain said that hour had to be done whatever time I came in, so I said to our Sergeant, "Well, let us get on with it." We started, but the other two were hopeless cases, the Sergeant having me first at one end to show them fixing and then at the other to show them unfixing. This went on for about 15 minutes and I was getting fed up and disgusted, my mates chaffing me over it, when the Captain came up and said, "Let me see them do it, Sergeant."

Well, one of these new fellows went out when the order came, "Fix!" and made a terrible bungle of it.

The Sergeant said, "Get at the other end, Andrews," and I did the fix, which of course was all right - I could have done it in my sleep! Then he tried the second chap with "Unfix!" Same thing - he could not do it, so I was ordered back to the other end to do the unfix.

"You fall out, Andrews," said the Captain. "You two stop here for an hour, and an hour every night until you can do it."

So I went and sat down to watch them taught it. I know I thought, "If that is going on guard with men off a draft, I want no more." I had completely lost my temper.

It was at Riencourt we did the attack in front of all the Generals, the aeroplanes being out with us as well.

23 (21) Jun 1916: One morning I was wakened very early and told to pack up - we were moving. I noticed my mates weren't putting their overcoats in and asked them where they were. "Oh, we gave them in at midnight last night. The transport is carrying them as it is a long march we are going to do." So I had to carry full kit and a few extra things I had promised the Sergeant I would take for him. I had no time to bother about someone else taking the extra things now, so I set off with the lot.

We had covered a few miles when our Colonel came riding alongside the Battalion and as he was passing me, said, "How is it you are carrying full kit?" I told him I was asleep when the order was given and had not been wakened. "Do you think you will manage it?" I said I was going to try!

By the time we had marched through Breilly, Ailly sur Somme and Amiens (about 20 miles) I was about beat, but I dared not fall out because of the extra things I was carrying - it would have given the Sergeant away. It was a very hot day and by the time we reached Corbie about 6.00pm I was past tired and it took me all my time to get up some stairs. The last few miles I had been staggering along like a drunken man.

24 [22] Jun 1916: The next morning I was charged for falling out on the left hand side of the road without permission. "What have you got to say, Andrews?" asked our Captain - Mather was his name.

I said, "I did what I thought was best."

A dump for salvaged cartridge cases behind the lines

"Yes, I know you did, and you have been in the Battalion long enough to know different. Seven days CB."

About four o'clock the same day we marched off again, going by the lower road towards Bray once more. Half way we had to halt until it was dark so that the Germans could not see us. I was still carrying full kit but no extra. I had not got over the march of the day before and by midnight I was simply tumbling along. I said, "I am falling out," but the Officer heard me and said, "Don't. You only have a mile to go." He didn't want any more falling out - nearly half our Platoon had gone already, three collapsing completely. And they weren't carrying full kit, so you can imagine how I felt! All I got told was I had proved I was a soldier!

As soon as we got to the billet, rations had to be drawn and it was my turn. I went with three others to the stores and got the bacon to carry but did not carry it far before I sat down on the side of the road. It was no use - I was beat and could not do any more. One of our cooks came up and carried it for me - he had been riding, so was quite fresh.

Before the Attack

We stayed here at Etinehem two days, with me still doing extra fatigues for my CB. We had a lecture from the doctor on how to bandage wounds and so on, and a Church service in which we were told that Christ gave up his life for others; we were about to go forward and some of us would be called upon to make that great sacrifice - about a 15 minute sermon.

The regimental history gives the move to Bray as next day, 23rd June. The following compromise would make sense: they arrived at Etinehem on the night of Friday 23rd June and stayed there on Saturday 24th and Sunday 25th, moving to Bray on the Sunday evening. There is no discrepancy in dates for the following week and the lecture and service suggest a longer stop than one night. The service could well have been on the Sunday and it would seem logical for such preparations to be made outside Bray, which was crowded.

Well, we left Etinehem for Bray and here we were getting ready to go up to the trenches to do the attack. The bombardment had been on from Sunday, June 25th. You could hear nothing but a roar of guns day and night, and we were six miles from the firing line.

We already had one colour on the back of our tunics, a green and yellow star, which was the Battalion colour. Now we had to stick a yellow cloth over the flap of our pack - I believe this was for the Artillery Observing Officer to see in the attack how far we had got. On top of this went a tin disc for the aeroplanes to see to signal where we were to our Artillery. We had already been wearing short trousers all the summer. These had to be just above the knee and the puttees just below, showing our bare knees, which was all right in the daytime but not at night. Anyway I had a piece of red ribbon which I had to sew round the bottom of the right trouser leg with a bow on the outside. This was to show I was entitled to go down German dugouts after clearing out.

Mon 26/Tue 27 Jun 1916: We had a new Officer who had just come out from England and had only been with us about a fortnight. When we paraded he asked me if I had had a shave that morning and I said yes. "Take his name, Sergeant, for not shaving." The next morning

Heavy artillery on the Somme front

it was the same question and the same answer.
After the parade the Sergeant asked me about it and I said, "I want a new razor."
"Well," he said, "that is two crimes against you and you are doing 7 days now."
I was - my job that Tuesday was filling petrol tins all day with water, ready to be carried to us in the attack. I said, "It will be the same in the morning unless you get me a new razor."

28 Jun 1916: On the Wednesday we drew picks and shovels, bombs and an extra 150 rounds of ammunition. That afternoon a few of us went for a swim in the River Somme, putting our clothes on the side. We had not been in the water long when a storm came on and we had to do a dash to the bank to get our clothes. Of course, they were wet through! We got back to the billet soaked to the skin and were told that the attack had been postponed for 48 hours. [The decision to postpone from Thursday 29th June until Saturday 1st July was taken at eleven o'clock on the Wednesday morning.]

We gave our picks and shovels in, but first we had to parade to have everything inspected and of course I got my name taken again for not shaving. The Sergeant said, "This is three times, Andrews."
"I don't care if it is forty-three," I replied. "We are going over the top on Saturday anyway."

Thur 29 Jun 1916: He got me a new razor and when I paraded next morning, the Officer had a very close look at my face and said, "Oh, you have shaved this morning." We were not allowed to speak back to an Officer or I would have told him that when he had seen as much service as my razor he would not be so sharp. I felt like hitting him on the head with it, I was so disgusted. He must have thought he was still show soldiering!

We had to draw picks and shovels again that morning, and rations for two days. Bray that week was simply packed with French and British troops and no-one was allowed out or in, which meant there was nothing you could buy after a day or two. There were dozens of our observation balloons up and a church service was held every day at noon.

About 5.00pm we paraded and marched off through our guns. We had to be guided over some of the hills as the shells from our guns were only clearing them by three feet. It was going through these that we were nearly blinded by gas shells. Our Artillery lads watching us go by were saying they would look after us on Saturday - "We'll give them hell!" - and the Frenchmen were working at the 75mm guns like niggers, smiling and shouting to us as we passed.

We arrived in the support line about 8.00pm and I was put on sentry with two others to look for anything unusual happening, strange lights and so on. By now, of course, I knew all the usual lights - red, green and so on - that the Germans threw up. The noise from our guns was deafening.

That night we went up to the front line after a good rum issue, our bombers doing a raid about 11.00pm. The guns were now roaring worse than ever and to speak to anyone you had to get close to their ear and shout at the top of your voice. But I was tired and fell asleep sitting on a firestep with my overcoat over my head. [The bombardment began at 11.05pm, the raid to get prisoners at 11.20. The party found the German front line deserted and levelled by the bombardment. They returned at 11.40 with one wounded, one killed of the 39 who went out.]

Fri 30 Jun 1916: The next day an Officer came and asked what I was there for. I told him I was on sentry and he said, "Do you see that red house?"
Yes," I said.
"There is a German sniper in there."
"Yes," I said, to get rid of him. There was no red house on the front and he was obviously what a soldier would call "puddled", meaning mixed up.

A French "75" and its ammunition wagon

The Battle of the Somme

All this activity was leading up to one of the most notorious dates in the history of warfare, 1st July 1916. The British Third and Fourth Armies, disposed along a wide front stretching from Gommecourt in the north to Maricourt in the south, were to attack at the same time as the French Sixth Army, which was positioned on their right astride the Somme. The object was to relieve pressure on the French at Verdun and to gain possession of the ridge of high ground stretching from Montauban to the River Ancre. The good observation afforded by this ridge might make it possible to penetrate the German lines and by attacking their flank and rear, "roll them up" northwards. Alternatively, if further advance proved impossible, the ridge would be relatively easy to hold while the attack was switched to another front.

The plan required an advance of 4,000 yards in the first day and the preliminary bombardment was designed to smash the wire and the German defences beforehand. In most places, it failed to do so. The bad weather of the last week of June made both observation and range-finding difficult, even after it was decided to postpone the attack for 48 hours. Many shells were faulty and the German dugouts were deep.

The zero hour of 7.30am was a compromise: the British had wanted the cover of darkness and the French good light for their superior artillery. On 1st July the weather cleared. Slow-moving lines of men, weighed down as Albert Andrews describes and frequently held up by uncut wire, made excellent targets as they advanced across the bare landscape. Not until 13th July did the British Fourth Army reach a position from which it could attack the German second line. By then 60% of the officers and 40% of the men who took part in the attack had become casualties.

The casualty figures for the 19th Manchesters on 1st July were 187 men and 3 officers killed, wounded or missing. In contrast to what had happened elsewhere on the front, their action had been a brilliant success. Congreve was a careful general and the planning and training beforehand had been most thorough. The bombardment in that section had been more successful in knocking out the German artillery, too. The elation in Albert Andrews' account is understandable; he and his friends did not realise until later the extent of the slaughter elsewhere.

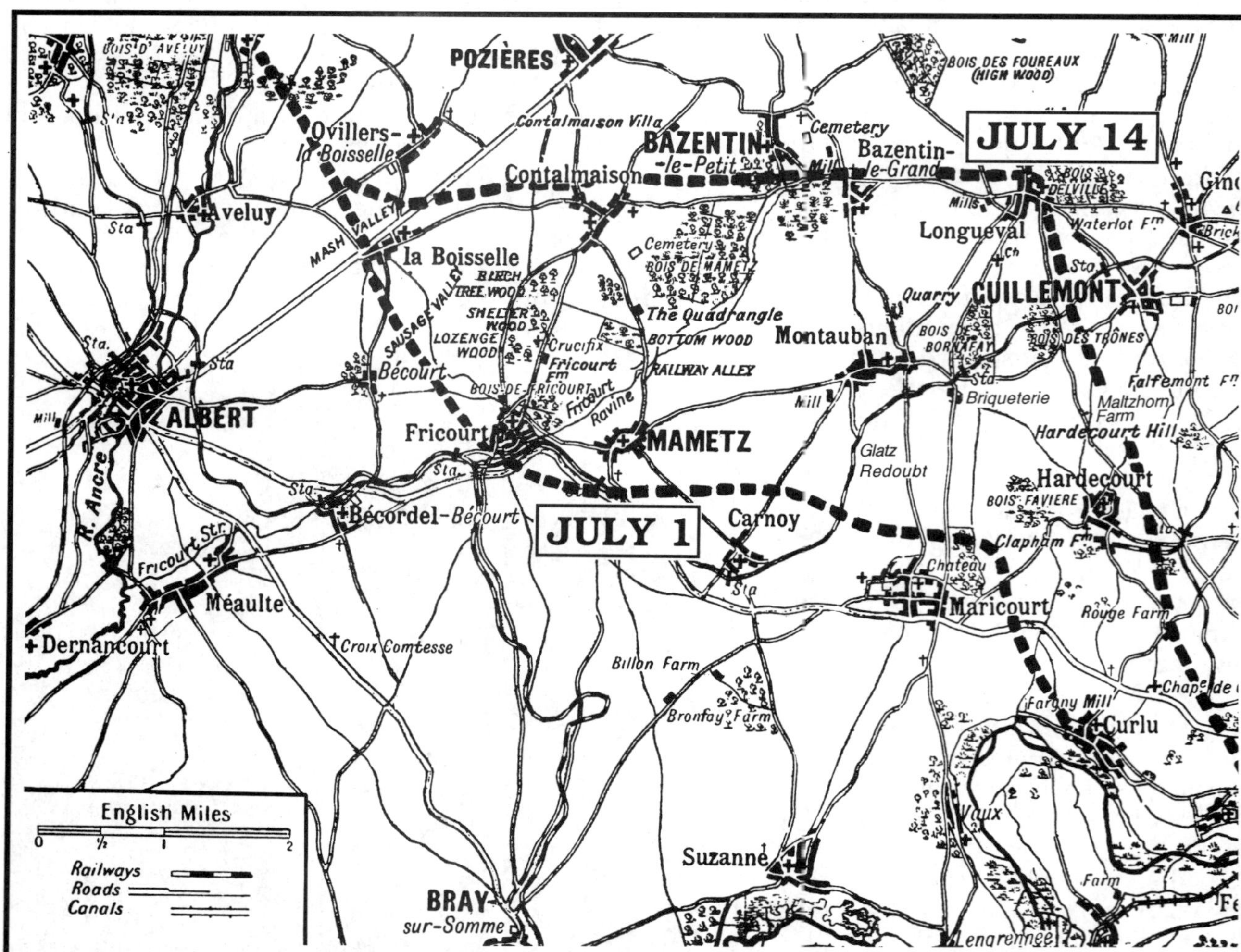

The Allied advance on the Somme between 1st July and 14th July 1916. The 19th Manchesters took Glatz Redoubt within their allotted time, allowing the 90th Brigade to go forward and capture Montauban. Albert Andrews was wounded in an attack on Guillemont on 23rd July

The First of July

Sat 1 Jul 1916: I was wakened about 5.00am for breakfast - dry bread, cheese and a drink of water. After breakfast we were putting over our trenches bridges ready made by the RE, fixing ladders for us to get out of our trench and taking our barbed wire down. Our Colonel came down the trench and asked us if we knew what time zero was.
"No, Sir."
"Well, it is 7.30. Anyone got a watch? It is 13 minutes past 6. Put your watches right and don't forget, be ready." A mist was on at this time but it cleared away about 6.45, then the rum was issued. I received less this time than I had ever received.

I will here tell what I carried: rifle and bayonet with a pair of wire cutters attached; a shovel fastened on my back; pack containing two days' rations, oilsheet, cardigan, jacket and mess tin; haversack containing one day's iron rations and two Mills bombs; 150 rounds of ammunition; two extra bandoliers containing 60 rounds each, one over each shoulder; a bag of ten bombs.

The orders came down:
"Half an hour to go."
"Quarter of an hour to go."
"Ten minutes to go."
"Three minutes to go."
I lit a cigarette and up the ladder I went.

There was a section to a ladder and you waited until the others got up in line. Each company formed a wave, so a Battalion formed four waves, each of about 250 men in line about one yard apart. [This differs slightly from the regimental history, which says A and C Companies formed waves 1, 2 and 3 between them; B Company waves 4 and 5 and D Company wave 6.]

At 7.30am on a beautiful sunny morning off we started, about 50 yards between each wave. I was carrying my rifle by the sling on my shoulder with the bayonet parallel to my ear and had not gone many yards, when whizz! - I felt as if someone had pulled at the top. However, I took no notice as we were at a quick march and it was taking us all our time to keep going. Like nearly every other fellow, I was smoking. No Man's Land was one mass of shell holes, the soil was loose and we had 400 yards of this to go to the first German trench.

Fritz let us have it with shrapnel, machine guns and rifles. As we travelled along our lads kept falling killed and wounded, and about half way across the second wave catches up with the first to fill these gaps up. About 100 yards from the German trench, our Officer turned and said, "Up a bit on the left," then pitched forwards. That was the last order he ever gave.

[This was probably 2/Lt Outram, who had joined the Battalion on 7 June. He was the only officer of B Company to appear in the casualty list (as missing). By the time B Company reached the gorge of Glatz Redoubt, sections were being taken to replace men killed or wounded in the first three waves.]

As we got nearer, dozens of Germans were running through us towards our lines with their hands up. Others stopped there throwing bombs, firing machine guns and rifles, but those who stayed until we got there will fire no more - well, very few.

I jumped into the German trench, what was left of it, just near a dugout door. In the doorway there was a big barrel. As soon as I jumped in, a German leapt from behind the barrel but I was already on guard and I had my bayonet on his chest. He was trembling and looked half mad with his hands above his head, saying something to me which I did not understand. All I could make out was that he did not want me to kill him! It was here I noticed my bayonet was broken and I couldn't have

"Three minutes to go"

stuck him with it. Of course, I had "one up the chimney" as we called it - that is, a bullet in the breech, so that you only have to press your trigger. I pointed to his belt and bayonet. He took these off, and his hat and water bottle as well, emptied his pockets and offered the lot to me.

Just then one of my mates was coming up the trench. "Get out of the way, Andy. Leave him to me, I'll give him one to himself" - he meant he would throw a bomb at him, which would have blown him to pieces.
"Come here," I said. He was on his knees in front of me now, fairly pleading. I said, "He's an old man" - he looked sixty.

At the finish I pointed my thumb towards our lines, never taking my bayonet off his chest. He jumped up and with his hands above his head ran out of the trench towards our lines, calling out all the time. He was trembling from head to foot and frightened to death. I honestly believe he could have done me as I jumped into the trench if he had not been so afraid. This was the only German I ever let off and I have never regretted it because I believe he could have done me quite easily.

Well, him away, we both bombed the dugout and turned round to go along the trench, when three fine Germans came running towards us with their hands up. They would be about 20 yards away. We both fired and two fell, my mate saying as he let go, "That's for my brother in the Dardanelles," and, as he fired again and the third German fell, "That's for my winter in the trenches." We walked up to them and one moved. My mate kicked him and pushed his bayonet into him. That finished him.

Of course, all this occurred in about five minutes, it taking a good deal longer to tell than do, and there were other instances, but I am just giving what I was actually involved in. This kind of thing was going on all along the line, no Germans being spared. Wounded were killed by us all. We hadn't exactly been told, "No prisoners," but we were given to understand that that was what was wanted. The same kind of thing occurred at the second German trench, and the third.

Then we waited outside Glatz Redoubt, all our guns being turned on this ring of trenches which was right on top of the ridge. We got the order "Charge!" and away we went at the double, killing all that stayed there. A good many retreated towards Montauban and we opened rapid fire at them.

The Taste of Victory

Well, our objective was reached. We had done all that had been asked of us and turned round to look where we had come from. We saw the 90th Brigade - the 16th, 17th and 18th Manchesters and one Battalion of the Scotch Fusiliers - approaching and let go rapid fire into Montauban to cover them while they were advancing. Owing to heavy machine gun fire, the Brigade was held up near us while our Artillery shelled Montauban, and they did! The village went down like a box of bricks. At five minutes to ten this Brigade was told to advance and then we had to cease fire as they were in front of us. We watched them, seeing them fall. I had my brother in this Brigade and wondered if he was one of those falling or not.

Just then our Colonel came.
"What Company are you?"
"B, Sir."
"Good," he said. "Make way," and off he went. He sent word back a few minutes later that the 90th Brigade had taken Montauban.

Then I was sent clearing dugouts. I know I was going

"The village went down like a box of bricks." Devastation at Montauban following its capture by the 90th Brigade on 1st July

over a bit of loose ground where the trench was blown down, when I heard someone call out, "Get down!" Of course, I did not want telling twice, then they called to me to go over there on my stomach as there was a sniper there. I crawled over and looked down at the bottom of this bit of a hill and then saw it was a timely warning, there being several of our fellows dead there at the bottom that this sniper had caught. Here I was sent back with a message to tell our Battalion that the Liverpools had gained all their objectives.

Two or three of us went down in a fine German dugout. There were cigars, tinned food and German helmets. We all took a helmet, cigars and tobacco and coming out with these German helmets on we ran right into our Captain. "Yes," he said, "you all look very nice, but get some ****ing digging done!" and sent us nearly as far as Montauban, up a communication trench which joined our Battalion with the 90th Brigade.

We were making this trench into a fire trench and a Corporal and I started to dig a firestep. I had been digging a bit until about mid-day and was hot and sweating.
"Let me have a go," said the Corp. I did and had a smoke, then asked him should I have another go? "No," he said.
"Well, shall I go and borrow a spade?"
"Yes," he said and off I went.
The Germans began to shell us very heavily and now shells were bursting all about. I got the spade, but while I was away a shell had dropped right on the spot where I had left the Corp and a machine gun team digging an emplacement for their gun. Every one was killed or wounded, the Corp I had left being killed.

I made my way back to my Platoon and here I was set

19th Manchesters

Casualties 1 July 1916

b = birthplace as listed in *Soldiers Died in the Great War*
All were listed as killed in action unless stated otherwise

12512 Pte Albert Edward Appleyard	b Ardwick
12002 Pte William Penrock Atkinson	b and lived Scarborough
12006 Cpl Arthur Baldwin	b Reddish
12005 Pte Fred Bannister	b Farington, Preston lived Leyland
12735 Pte Frank Bennett	b Manchester
12273 Pte William Blair	b Ancoats
12014 Pte Eric Blaydon	b Earlsfield, Middlesex lived Winnipeg
11480 Pte John Howard Bott	b and lived Ramsbottom
12877 Pte Albert Edward Bratby	b Congleton
26547 Pte Albert Cass	b Manchester
12296 Pte George Chadaway	b Collyhurst
11506 Sgt Walter Ashworth Chadwick	b Newton Heath *(died of wounds)*
11507 Sgt Leonard Charnock	b Fairfield, lived Reddish
12040 Pte Albert Clegg	b Miles Platting lived Warrington
12042 Pte Vernon Collinge	b Broughton
12314 Pte George Davies	b Miles Platting
25035 Pte Harold Davies	b Manchester, lived Oldham
12063 Pte Norman Labrow Dawes	b Rusholme
25073 Pte Hubert Dixon	b Oldham
11528 Pte Arthur Duckworth	b Whitefield
12074 Pte George Ernest Evans	b Manchester
11537 Pte Samuel Fallows	b Heywood
12729 Pte Fred Farnworth	b Manchester, lived Pendlebury
12733 Pte Samuel Freer	b Manchester
12343 Pte Harold Grant	b Salford, lived Stretford
11821 Cpl Raymond Hayes Grimshaw	b Wilmslow, lived Handforth
12368 L/Cpl William Percival Harper	b and lived Stockport
12099 Pte Marshall Heaton	b Middleton, lived Chester
12111 A/Cpl George Holt	b Longsight
12369 Pte William Howarth	b Hulme
12533 Pte Alfred Johnson	b Manchester
12124 Pte Ernest Eaton Jones	b Ardwick
12130 Pte Wilfred Thomas Larmour	b Levenshulme, lived Reddish
12714 Pte John Thomas Lloyd	b Salford
12390 Pte William Edward Lowry	b Cheetham
11599 Cpl Albert Lucas	b Old Trafford
12139 Pte Henry McDonald	b Moss Side
11612 Pte Edmund Mellor	b and lived Oldham
11614 Sgt Arthur Mitchell	b Hemsworth, Yorks
26851 Pte Charles Herbert Ollerenshaw	b Macclesfield
12420 Pte George Arthur Oxley	b Stretford
12556 Pte Charles John Parry	b Manchester
12542 Pte Emmanuel Radcliffe	b and lived Middleton
18477 Pte George Russell	
12800 Pte Samuel Shimwell	b Levenshulme
12203 Pte Albert Vincent Siddall	b Chorlton on Medlock
11685 Pte John Taylor	b Radcliffe
12224 Pte Walter Toole	b Manchester, lived Cornbrook *(died of wounds)*
26691 Pte Thomas Birchenall Tress	b Manchester, lived Harpurhey
26621 Pte Edward Vaughan	b and lived Bury
12234 Pte Thomas Ward	b Bury
12238 Pte John Welby	b Ancoats
11953 Pte Robert West	b Edgworth
12242 Pte Samuel Handley Whitfield	b Lower Broughton
11962 L/Cpl Robert Henry Wilkinson	b Stretford *(died of wounds)*
12493 Pte George Williams	b Bromsgrove, Worcs lived Bradford, Manchester
31070 Pte Arthur Windle	b Salford
12476 L/Cpl Albert Alfred Wollen	b Bristol lived Newtown, Bristol
12650 Pte George Woolridge	b Walsall, Staffs
17807 Pte Frederick Wright	b Crewe

digging again. A shell was coming and all ducked that could, one of my mates getting a piece in the back. He was bandaged up but was groaning.

I leaned over him and started talking to him, trying to persuade him he was all right, but every minute he would call out, "Andy, give me a drink," then "Andy, ease me," "Andy, it does hurt. Why don't they move me and take this out of my back?" He then complained about it being hot and the sun in his eyes, so I put my khaki handkerchief over his face. I could hardly stand to see the agony written on his face.
Two or three asked, "Could we not carry him down?"
No, we must not stir.

By this time it was sickening. Everywhere you looked there were dead and wounded, the Germans doing us while we were digging in. I was giving this boy a drink when the Colonel came along. This would be about 6.00pm, I should think. The Colonel asked me where he was hit and how long he had been there and I told him, "About five hours." About an hour later our Battalion Doctor came up with stretcher bearers. I heard him saying he had not stopped one minute all the day, the RAMC being late or something. He looked at this boy, shook his head and the lad was carried away. He died, I believe, on the stretcher going down.

Ten of the 19th Manchesters 1st July casualties. Left to right, from the top: Pte William Blair, aged 21, lived in Palmerston Street, Ancoats and worked at Newton Street Post Office. Pte Norman Dawes had family living in Beech Road, Sale. A/Cpl George Holt lived in Dickenson Road, Longsight. Pte Alfred Johnson lived in Clito Street in Moston and worked for Affleck & Brown, Oldham Street, Manchester. Pte Walter Toole (died of wounds) lived in Ogden Street, Cornbrook. Pte William Edward Lowry lived in Bower Street, Broughton, and was a printer with the CWS in Longsight. He was a well known local footballer and was in the team which won the Pals Cup at Heaton Park. Pte Charles Ollerenshaw, aged 28, lived in Ackroyd Street, Higher Openshaw and worked for Armstrong Whitworth. Pte George Arthur Oxley, aged 21, lived in Pattens Street, Withington, and worked for Richard Goodair Ltd (merchants) of Mosley Street, Manchester. Pte Charles John Parry, aged 30, lived in Carlton Street, Rusholme, and worked for Andrew & Co (insulated cables), Whitworth Street West. Pte Samuel Shimwell lived in Elbow Street, Levenshulme

Then for the first time some others and I had something to eat. A Yorks Captain came up, saying, "Pleased to see you here, boys. I have been in this war since it began but that was the prettiest sight I have seen, you boys set off to the Germans smoking and walking and keeping line."

The following section has been adapted slightly to tally with dates given in the regimental history. The original account gives: 2nd July - all day digging: Monday 3rd July - relief by the South Africans and to the front line trench; carrying stores and burying parties. This seems rather a lot to fit in on one day and the sentence "We spent all next day digging" is vague, as if he isn't quite sure of the time scale at this point.

If the move to the (old) front line trench was, as stated in the history, after the relief by the King's Liverpools, then Sunday would be spent digging and carrying stores and wire in the new advanced positions. The burial parties would have been sent out from the old assembly trenches on the Monday, before the relief by the South Africans at 5.30pm.

Sat 1/Sun 2 Jul 1916: I only did one hour's sentry that night. The Germans counter-attacked but were repulsed. We spent all next day digging and carrying wire and all kinds of trench stores. Luckily the German shellfire had eased a bit. [At 10.00pm on the 2nd] we were relieved [by the 20th King's Liverpools], but we did not go far away, only to our own front line trench.

Mon 3 Jul 1916: On the Monday I was put with others burying the dead and this was when we realised the cost of our victory.

The first Tuesday the roll was called there were too many that did not answer. Burying your own lads is not a job that I want again, some seeming by their looks to have died very easy, others very hard. Some we had to dig out - they had been half buried. The job consisted of getting hold of them, taking their equipment off and emptying their pockets. You put the contents in the gas helmet satchel and hand this to the Officer who is with you, giving the man's name, number and Regiment if possible. Then they are put into a hole ready dug with boots and everything on. You put in about 10 or 15, whatever the grave will hold, throw about two feet of earth on them and stick a wooden cross on the top which is marked by the Officers. For some it was the third day and you could hardly stand the stench as you got hold of them, often having to put them down, go out of the way and have a smoke. The game wanted sticking!

Burial

On Monday night we were relieved by the 9th Division - South Africans, they were - and we went back to Etinehem Wood. I know as we passed through our guns our Artillery gave us a right good cheer and the road to Etinehem was lined with British and French troops cheering us. Nearly every one of us had something German.

[Fri 7 Jul] 1916: My brother Tom came to Etinehem to see if I had come through it and I was very pleased to see him. I had no idea how he had gone on, but I could not get to know as while he was with me orders came: "Pack up." We were off again, to take a wood, we were told. We had not got clear of the battle yet. Anyway, Friday night found us back again with a lot of fresh men; a draft had been waiting for us.

The success of XIII Corps in the early stages of the Somme battle brought its own problems. They now held a narrow section of front with unprotected flanks. Rawlinson had stressed the need to consolidate the first objectives

Manchesters resting near Mametz, July 1916

gained and General Horne, commanding XV Corps on Congreve's left, had refused to move forward, despite reports that Mametz Wood was empty. On the other hand, the French were pressing for a further advance and on 3rd and 4th July Trones Wood was reported to be unoccupied. General Congreve, naturally cautious, decided to stay where he was.

The decision proved costly. The German army in that sector had been much depleted on 1st July, but the British delay in following through gave them time to bring up reinforcements. Thus, the attack of 8th July in which Albert Andrews was involved proved inconclusive and Trones Wood remained in dispute until after the 30th Division had left the area. The wood was important, for it was on the right flank of the next planned attack, and on 12th July the commander of 18th Division was told to take it "even if it takes your whole Division".

The capture of Guillemont was to be even more difficult. It was necessary to control this village if the next advance was to be aligned with the French, but it was strongly defended and the approach from Trones Wood was across open country. After the 19th Manchesters' attempt on 23rd July, there were repeated assaults in August and the village eventually fell to the 59th Brigade on 3rd September.

Two of the 19th Manchesters who died of their wounds after 1st July: Pte George Woodbridge Thomas, aged 21, lived in Crondall Street, Moss Side, and worked for W R Howarth & Co (publishers) of Manchester. Pte Joseph Thomas Lane, aged 19, lived in Frank Street, Oldham

19th Manchesters

Casualties 2 - 8 July 1916

b = birthplace as listed in *Soldiers Died in the Great War*
KIA = Killed in Action. DoW = Died of Wounds

11986 Pte George W Thomas	b Moss Side	DoW 2 July
25066 Pte Joseph Thomas Lane	b Liverpool	DoW 3 July
11815 Pte James Gilman	b Salford	DoW 3 July
12845 Pte James Hillen	b and lived Bolton	DoW 3 July
12428 Pte Stanley Pearce	b Ardwick	DoW 3 July
12660 Pte Owen Joseph Clancey	b Carrick on Shannon, Roscommon, Ireland	DoW 4 July
12129 Cpl Albert D Knighton	b Kentish Town, Middlesex lived Coventry	DoW 4 July
12155 Pte Frederick James Moss	b Glossop	DoW 5 July
12328 Pte Edwin Stanley Fenton	b Heywood	KIA 8 July
12467 Pte David Thomas	b Bethesda, Carnarvon	DoW 8 July

Trones Wood - Shellshocked

Sat 8 Jul 1916: The [2nd] Yorks made the attack on Trones Wood early on the Saturday morning. We were in Glatz Redoubt as their supports. The Yorks were repulsed in this attack with heavy loss, few of them being left. About 9.00am this morning we were just going to have breakfast when the Sergeant warned six of us to go back for water and rum. Going down a trench called Train Alley - this was where our Brigadier's dugout was - we heard him saying on the 'phone that he was going to withdraw the Yorks and send the 19th Manchesters to attack with the [2nd] Wilts.

It had been raining about two days then, the trenches were full of water and we were plastered with mud. Anyway we got the water and rum all right and were making our way back when one of the Officers came and said, "Put those tins down and get back as quick as you can. Put your packs on - we are going over at one o'clock." Of course we knew, having overheard our General on the 'phone. Anyway we had to leave the water and the rum and go and get our packs on. We just had time to do this before we left Glatz Redoubt and moved off, making our way towards a place called the Briqueterie. As we passed it, the Germans were shelling us very heavily and a "coal box" (a shell) dropped right in front of four of us, wounding or killing three. I "went skating" with the concussion; how I was missed I cannot tell - it must not have been my turn. When I caught up with my mates, someone said, "Here's Andy. We thought you had gone." I know I never answered or spoke until we got into a sunken road in front of Trones Wood.

Here the Germans shelled us for all they were worth. One of our Captains said, "Three minutes to go, lads," walked about 15 yards and fell, hit in the head. He died, I hear, being carried down on the stretcher. [Captain Royle of D Company appears in the casualty lists. He was one who had gone overseas with the original Battalion in 1915.]

Well, over we went and the Wilts took the wood except the top corner; this fight swayed to and fro. Here our Platoon finished just on the right of the wood, joining up with the French. The Germans gave it us hot here and our lads kept

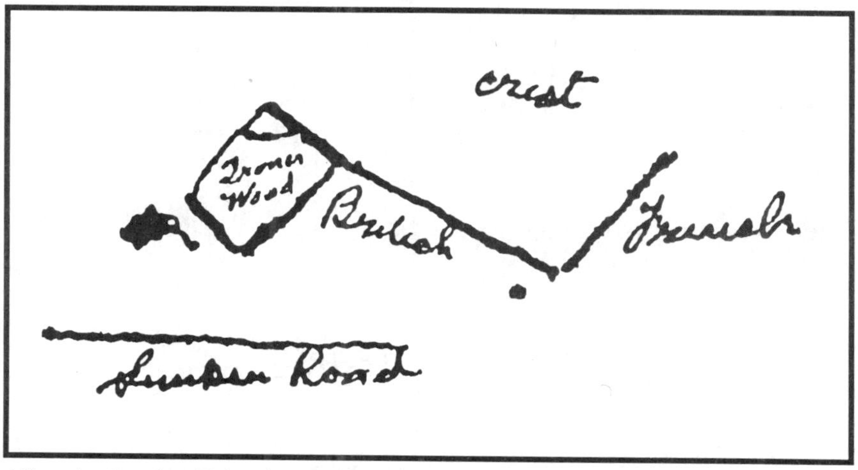

Albert's sketch of his platoon's position at Trones Wood

tumbling one by one. I would have given anything for a drink of water, but there was none to be had. About 5.00pm I had just come down from doing an hour's sentry and had got some food, about to have my first proper meal since the night before, when "Stand to!" came down the line. They were coming, but it was only a weak affair.

A French Captain came talking to a few of us as we were digging. We asked him where the Germans were and he said the main troops were about a mile away, but they had left some digging nearer and some in a farm. They came over again and one of us asked if he thought they would come back. He laughed and said he did not think so, but if they did they would be well received by the French "75s". He said, laughing and pointing to some bushes on the right, "They know them from Verdun."

About 9.00pm a mate and I were digging and we dug a dead German up; he must have been buried alive. We soon covered him up again, the stench nearly knocking us down! Just then our Sergeant came up and said someone had to go and lie out on the top of the crest in front. I looked and said, "What a nice job for someone!"
"You will be one, Andy," he replied. I stopped digging, turned round and asked why.
"Well," he said, "I cannot send any of these new lads," and pointed out how few of us there were - about four of us, I think, knew what we were doing - and it was the Captain's orders.
"When have I to go out?" I asked.
"Ten o'clock. I will warn you and put three new ones half way." I stopped digging, sat down in the trench and started smoking. I admit I did not like this job I was going on, but anyway at ten or soon after out I went and lay there. After a while I was brought in, but then had to go out again.

9 Jul 1916: This would be about 2.00am. It was very dark and I had been told not to shoot at the first thing I saw as the French were sending a patrol out. This made my position very awkward. I had to wait until someone was on top of me to find out in the dark whether they were Germans or French, but my mind was made up on this point. That French patrol did not come near me and I think it was a good thing for one of them at least.

Ruins of a village near Mametz

Between two and three the Germans counter-attacked just on our left and after a stiff fight were driven off. Trones Wood was simply lit up by shellfire that night.

When I came in, our Sergeant said, "We are going over again at dawn."

I looked and cursed. They were nearly all new troops. I had lost nearly all my old mates and was fed up myself.

Just before dawn the order came: "19th Manchesters, packs on." This would be Sunday morning, July 9th. A little while after came the order, "Right turn and file out of the trench."

19th Manchesters
Casualties 9-11 July 1916

b = birthplace as listed in *Soldiers Died in the Great War*
KIA = Killed in Action. DoW = Died of Wounds

11998 Pte Percy Anderson	b Broughton	DoW 9 July
11547 Pte Fred Holding Foy	b Bolton lived Gravesend, Kent	KIA 9 July
12327 L/Cpl Ernest French	b Longsight	KIA 9 July
12859 Pte Edwin Grist	b Manchester	KIA 9 July
12098 Sgt Ross Healey	b Swinton, lived Eccles	KIA 9 July
12355 Pte George Hurdle	b Moss Side	KIA 9 July
12376 L/Cpl Frank Jeffreys	b Patricroft	KIA 9 July
18488 Pte William Leech	b and lived Hyde	KIA 9 July
12402 Pte William Litherland	b and lived Salford	KIA 9 July
12392 Pte Edwin Broom Logan	b Ardwick	KIA 9 July
11644 Pte Frank Ramsbottom	b Pendleton lived Failsworth	KIA 9 July
11710 L/Sgt Jack George Yuill	b Willesden, lived Sale	KIA 9 July
12055 Pte William Crowe	b Harpurhey	DoW 11 July
11816 Cpl Ernest Godsall	b Gorton, lived Droylsden	DoW 11 July

The [2nd] Royal Scotch Fusiliers [90th Brigade] had come up during the night to do the attack on this farm (Maltzhorn Farm) instead of us - we were too weak. They relieved us and we went back to the support line, the whole 21st Brigade being relieved by the 90th.

Anxiety and Praise

This was all right for me, but I knew I had come out of a hot place and my brother was going into it. However, I fell asleep until dinner time, then had a feed and watched the Germans shell Trones Wood and Montauban; it looked as if nothing could live in those places. They were letting us have it too, but not so bad. During that afternoon we heard that the 90th Brigade were losing very heavily and could see the wounded coming down, some walking, others on trucks one on top of the other like sheep. My brother had been fighting with them and I was wondering where he was.

At night we had to rush about getting fitted up again with bombs and ammunition. The 90th Brigade were very weak owing to heavy losses and might call on us if the Germans counter-attacked. We lay in wait until it went dark, all of us having had enough of it. During this attack the Germans used a great many gas shells and I had my eyes closed above once with these. At 10.15 we moved back to Billon Wood. The Germans had evidently had enough as well!

We stayed in Billon Wood a few days, going up burying our dead and carrying wire, water and ammunition to the troops in the fire trench. On one of these days we were sitting having our tea when our C/O came and asked what Company we were. We told him B Company. "I have just received a message from your Commander-in-Chief. I will read it. 'You have covered yourselves with glory'," he said. "Tell the other Companies, tell the Brigade, Division, tell the whole British Army!" and the Major stood there and said, "I am proud of the company I am in."

Soon after this I was told my brother was wounded and missing. This upset me more than all the fighting, but later I saw what was left of their Battalion coming out and asked

Four of the 19th Manchesters casualties, 9 and 11 July. From top left: Pte William Litherland lived in Lowcock Street, Lower Broughton, and worked for the Manchester & Liverpool Bank in Spring Gardens, Manchester. Pte Frank Ramsbottom lived in Dean Street, Failsworth, and worked for the Fine Cotton Spinners' & Doublers' Association in Manchester. Pte William Crowe, aged 24, lived in Hall Street, Moston, and worked for W H Milner & Co (wine & spirit merchants), Pall Mall, Manchester. L/Sgt Jack George Yuill lived in Wardle Road, Sale, and worked for Henry Blacklock & Co (publishers), Albert Square. He was a well known amateur footballer and captain of Northern Nomads FC

his Sergeant. He said he was wounded in the back, was just able to walk but was breathing very badly.

I said, "He is not missing, then?"
"No, he would get to the dressing station all right." This made me a little more contented. Tom was out of it, I thought.

[Sat 15 Jul] 1916: We had a train ride to a place called Saisseval but were only there about a day. Our Divisional General inspected us here and said he had come that day to thank us for what we had done. He said, "The 19th Manchesters had one hour to take Glatz Redoubt. They took it in 55 minutes. Before 7.30 that morning I was anxious, but when I saw the first waves go I was only sorry when I saw the wounded coming down. Such lads were too good to lose." He turned to our Colonel and said, "Sir H B Hill, I expect much of your men."

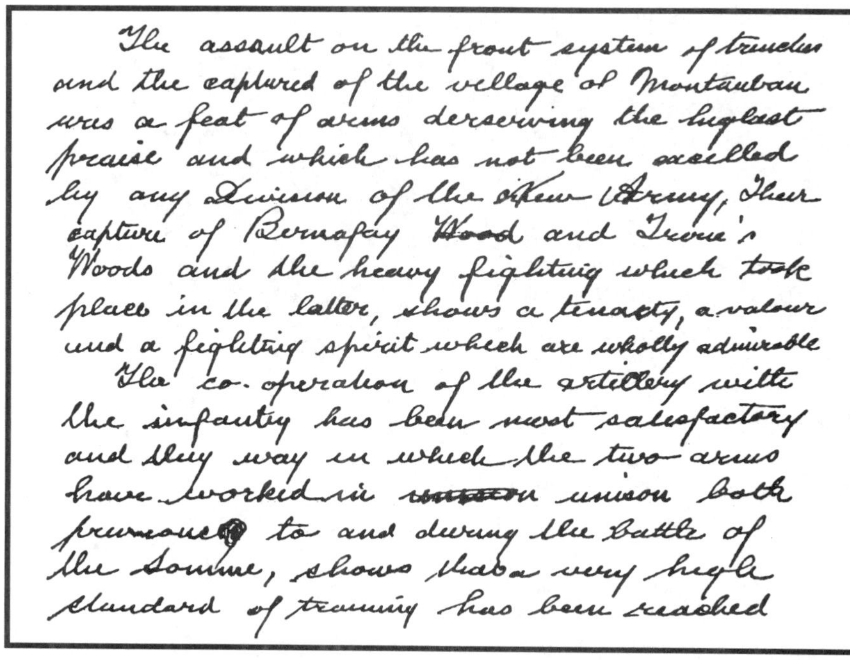
The assault on the front system of trenches and the captured of the village of Montauban was a feat of arms deserving the highest praise and which has not been excelled by any Division of the New Army, Their capture of Bernafay Wood and Trone's Woods and the heavy fighting which took place in the latter, shows a tenacity, a valour and a fighting spirit which are wholly admirable

The co-operation of the artillery with the infantry has been most satisfactory and they way in which the two arms have worked in unison both previous to and during the battle of the Somme, shows that a very high standard of training has been reached

An extract from the Army Commander's report of the Somme battle, quoted in the "Daily Dispatch" and proudly copied out by Albert Andrews in 1917

Then he spoke to the Division, saying the Division had done all that was asked of it and we should go back for a rest, but we had done so well we were being transferred from the XIII Army Corps to another and we were to be called upon again. "I have two messages here I will read to you which I, as your General, say you have earned. The first is from Sir Douglas Haig saying you have covered yourselves with glory. I am proud of that but still more proud of this one from the French Commander-in-Chief which says he wants the troops that were on his immediate left to be there again in his next general attack, as they inspired his troops to go on. 'Their

Troops resting near Mametz Wood

coolness under fire was remarkable and their bravery beyond praise.' I will place these two messages on the Manchester Regiment record. I am proud to be your General."

Movements according to the regimental history were as follows: 11th July - march to Morlancourt; 13th July - to Corbie; 14th July - march to Vecquemont, train to Ailly sur Somme, march to Saisseval for the GOC's Divisional address on 15th July; 18th July - via Ailly and Mericourt to billets at Morlancourt. 19th July: to Wellington Redoubt for training. Major General Shea had taken over as Divisional C/O in June. The transfer from the XIII Army Corps appears not to have taken place immediately. On 26th October the Battalion was transferred from the Fourth to the Third Army.

We went back on the train and

Morlancourt in 1918

into it again, stopping in front of Mametz; we were only getting about one slice of bread a day in our rations at this point.

A reserve trench near Guillemont

We were told we were going to attack a village. We saw one of our 'planes brought down over Mametz Wood, and then one of theirs down on the Saturday afternoon about three o'clock.

Guillemont - Wounded

Sat 22 Jul 1916: Soon after this we moved up to the first original German trench, stayed there until 10 o'clock and then up the Montauban road along the railway, the Germans shelling us and knocking our lads over like skittles. We were ordered to double.

Sun 23 Jul 1916: We arrived at Trones Wood about 11.00pm on Saturday night and from here attacked a village called Guillemont, which is situated in front of Combles. We attacked just before dawn, I being told off to carry a coil of barbed wire on a stake. We had 1,000 yards to go over the open. I soon dropped the barbed wire and lost the spade off my back - the Germans were waiting for us! After some hand to hand fighting we captured the village, but they counter-attacked immediately, cutting off our first two waves, who were all killed, wounded or taken prisoner; all the Officers in these first two waves are prisoners. The third and fourth waves suffered very heavily through this. There was only a handful of us and we had to withdraw at 6.00am.

I was shot through the right shoulder. A 2nd Wilts bandaged me with an extra field dressing I had got from the Sergeant before we went into it. He had asked me as he gave it me what I wanted two for. I said, "I don't fancy this," it being the first time in the battle I had any doubts. After I was bandaged I set off back over the 1,000 yards, but had not gone far before I found I was being sniped at, so worked the old soldier run as well as I could - stop, walk, fall. Doing this, however good a shot he is, he is lucky to hit you.

Well, I got back into Trones Wood into a trench and made my way to our doctor. He said, "Hello, have they hit you?" He bandaged me properly, put a ticket on me and said, "Blighty for you this time, Andrews. Can you walk down?" I was feeling faint but said I thought I could if he would give me a drink. I had this and set off down the railway line, passing Bernafay Wood and leaving Montauban on my right, asking for another drink all the way, but no, there was no water. Then I was put on a motor vehicle which put me down on the Bronfay road.

I was just about done now and was staggering along. I think I would have given up some time since, but my nose was towards home. A parson saw me nearly fall, picked me up and carried me into the dressing station at Billon Farm, where he gave me a drink of tea.

While I was drinking this, a General came, looked on my shoulder and said, "Manchesters," asking where I was wounded. I told him Guillemont.
He seemed as if he could hardly believe it until a Yorks said to him, "Yes, Sir, the Manchesters are in Guillemont."
He turned to me and said, "Are they in it now?"
I said, "They were when I left, but were being hard pressed in a counter-attack by the Germans." He waited for no more and off he went with some other Officers. I asked who he was, with him seeming so anxious, and was told it was General Rawlinson, he being our Army Commander.

Albert Andrews was never to rejoin the 19th Manchesters. About the middle of August, the Battalion moved up to the Bethune area and into the trenches at Givenchy, but in September they were back, and in October were involved in an attack on the Ligny-Thilloy ridge near Bapaume and in other action near Longueval. Most of November and December they spent near the Doullens/Arras road, in and out of the trenches near Berles au bois. With the British advance the following spring, the 19th Manchesters were centred on Henin sur Cojeul south-east of Arras and by April 24th they were near the Hindenburg line at Cherisy.

That summer they were transferred north and spent the rest of the year fighting in the area south of Ypres around Wytschaete and Zillebeke. At the end of January 1918 they were near St Quentin, but on 3rd February the whole army was reorganised to give three battalions to a brigade. The junior battalion of each brigade was disbanded, and the 19th Manchesters were the junior battalion. On 6th February, A and B Companies were transferred to the 16th Manchesters and C and D Companies to the 17th Manchesters.

A dressing station on the Montauban - Guillemont Road, 1916

19th Manchesters — Killed in action 23 July 1916

b = birthplace as listed in *Soldiers Died in the Great War*

11727 Pte Alan Davenport Adshead b Stockport, lived Heaton Chapel
12811 L/Cpl Bernard Harry Ashby b Derby, lived Southport
12279 Pte Charles Frederick Backhouse b and lived Oldham
31174 Pte William Edward Baker b Manchester, lived Ripon
11470 L/Cpl Charles Clifford Bate b Bury, lived Ramsbottom
11471 L/Cpl William Andrew Bayley b Manchester
26579 Pte William Edward Birkenhout b Miles Platting
12287 Pte Fred Blears b Pendleton
11749 Pte Harry Bold b Disley, lived Stockport
31177 Pte Alfred Bradbury b Manchester
17833 Pte Arthur Brady b and lived Barrow in Furness
26882 Pte Charles Brierley b Manchester
11491 Sgt William Brookes b and lived Swinton
12537 Pte James Lyndon Brown b Blackley
11492 Pte Joseph Brown b Salford
11768 Pte Richard Henry Brownbill b Ainsdale, lived Chorley
11493 Pte William Small Bruce b Hulme
12840 Pte William Wootton Bryans b Manchester
12793 L/Sgt Walter Butler b Collyhurst
12297 Pte Cyril Stanley Chadwick b and lived Salford
12298 Pte Cecil Chalmers b Bolton, lived Chorlton-on-Medlock
11509 Pte James Clowes b Macclesfield
25046 Pte William Collinge b Hollinwood
12300 Pte Edward Cook b Manchester
31076 Pte Henry Basil Craig b Manchester
12295 Pte Alfred Rudolph Craven b Manchester
26923 Pte Norman Currell b Withington
12315 L/Cpl John Vincent Standish Dawber b Pendleton
12319 Cpl Wilfred Dawson b and lived Middleton
31176 Pte Joseph Dodd b Salford
31165 Pte Francis James Dunn b and lived Buxton
12069 L/Cpl James Duxbury b Salford
12071 Cpl George Edward Edwards b Northants, lived Sussex
12076 Cpl Thomas Fairclough b Manchester
11539 Cpl Frank Fenton b Salford, lived Ansdell, Lytham
11806 Pte Thomas Henry Finch b Barrow in Furness
31156 Pte Edward Fitzpatrick b Manchester
26724 Pte Frank Fletcher b High Lane, Cheshire
12079 Pte Thomas Allan Foley b Gorton
31199 Pte Robert Samuel Friday b Manchester
11810 Pte John Fury b Rochdale
11811 Cpl Lees Garside b Hollinwood, lived Failsworth
12347 Pte Thomas Henry George b Thrupp, Stroud, Gloucs
12342 Pte Leonard Edward Gleadhill b and lived Beverley, Yorks
12333 Pte Percy Turner Glover b Birkenhead, lived Stockport
11555 Pte Thomas Glover b Openshaw
11563 Cpl George Gregory b Manchester
26531 Pte Joseph Gwyther b Manchester
12361 Pte John Hancock b Clayton
34049 Pte Frank Harding b Chadderton
12095 Pte Robert Harrison b Hulme, lived Salford
26725 Pte Alfred Heaton b Manchester
17922 Pte William E Higginbottom b Barrow in Furness, lived Stockport
12109 Pte James Holdsworth b Ardwick
12710 Pte Philip Henry Holmes b Manchester
33633 Pte John Hough b Manchester
33864 Pte George Henry Hulme b Manchester, lived Urmston
25053 Pte George Hurlston b Heyside, Royton
11858 Pte James Joseph Hynes b Dublin, lived Beswick
12547 Pte Harold Jackson b Manchester
12375 Pte Rupert Jevons b Chorlton
12816 Pte Samuel William Johnson b Salford
12374 Pte Albert Jones b and lived Denbigh
26928 Pte Frank Jones b and lived Crewe
11588 Pte William Henry Jones b Salford, lived Urmston
26521 Pte William Harold Kay b Manchester
25022 Pte Edward Kettle b Manchester
12395 A/Sgt Lawrence N Lambert b Bowdon, Cheshire, lived Kersal
34074 Pte Harry Leeming b Manchester
33830 Pte Arnold Lewis

From top, left to right: Sgt William Brookes of Swinton. Pte Norman Currell of Upper Lloyd Street, Moss Side. Pte Joseph Dodd of Brown Street, Queens Road. Pte Thomas Henry Finch of Percival Street, Newton Heath. Pte John Fury of Rowbotham Street, Miles Platting. Pte John Hancock of Bradford Street, Ancoats. Pte William Henry Jones of Princess Road, Urmston. Pte Harry Leeming of Junction Street, Hulme. Pte Harold Moe. His mother worked at the Royal Schools for the Deaf, Old Trafford. Pte Frank Myerscough of Broming Street, Beswick

Pte George Pilley of Gibson Street, Ardwick. Pte William Rothwell of Stockport Road, Levenshulme. Pte Arthur Royse of Wetherall Street, Hightown. Pte Walter Shawcross of Jackson Street, Stretford. Sgt Jack Sheasby of Monton Street, Moss Side. Pte Arthur Swetnam had relatives in Ashover Street, Gorse Hill, Stretford. Pte Arthur C Tomlinson of Kippax Street, Rusholme. Pte Cyril Watts of Cottenham Street, Chorlton on Medlock. Pte Albert Wilkinson; his brother lived in Beverley Street, Blackley. Cpl Arthur Williams of Duerden Street, Salford

12398 Pte William Lomas	b Weaste
26713 Pte Martin Lynch	b Milltown Malbay, Ireland
11600 Pte James Lyons	b Manchester
12407 Pte Frank Mackereth	b and lived Ambleside
12674 Pte John Mannion	b and lived Kilmovee, Ireland
11886 Pte George Edmund Mapley	b Harpurhey
25089 Pte Robert Marsden	b Royton
31157 Pte Arthur Mason	b Manchester
12412 Pte William McCluskey	b York
12143 Cpl William Alexander McKie	b Tunstall, Staffs, lived Stranraer
12144 Pte George McNamara	b Sale
26627 Pte Hugh Meredith	b Wrexham, lived Newton Heath
11606 Pte Harold Moe	b San Antonio, Texas
12414 Pte Edward Moorhouse	b Flixton
12663 Pte Tom Barker Morton	b Moss Side
26657 Pte Frank Dickinson Myerscough	b Prestwich, lived Beswick
11898 L/Sgt Thomas Ewart Norris	b Congleton, lived Blackpool
26518 Pte Robert Nuttall	b Droylsden
31105 Pte Fred Ogden	b Oldham
12601 Pte William Ogden	b Beswick
12802 Pte Frederick Cecil Orme	b Woolwich, Kent, lived Didsbury
12429 Sgt Frank Paterson	b Collyhurst
18098 Pte John Pedley	b Chorlton cum Hardy, lived Wilmslow
26141 Pte George Pilley	
12180 Sgt Sidney Poizer	b Broughton, lived Pendleton
12803 Pte Sydney Poyner	b Hartford, Cheshire
12552 Pte Victor John Edward Prickett	b London
31045 Pte Tom Atcherby Pugh	b Eccles, lived Bramhall
11643 L/Cpl Walter Ramsbottom	b Pendleton, lived Failsworth
11660 Pte David Reeves	b Miles Platting
11646 Pte James Arnold Reid	b Ardwick
18436 Pte Harry Renshaw	b Manchester
11657 Pte Thomas Riley	b and lived Marple Bridge
11650 Pte John Roberts	b Manchester
12571 Pte John Kendal Robinson	b and lived Preston
12436 Pte William Henry Rogers	b Pendleton, lived Moston
11920 Pte William Rothwell	b Longsight
12197 Pte Arthur Royse	b Higher Broughton
34041 Pte Morris Rubenstein	b Manchester, lived Cheetham
11659 Pte Robert Bradbury Russell	b and lived Bramhall
11661 Pte William Senior	b Newton Heath
11666 Pte Thomas Shaw	b Tottington, lived Bury
31209 Pte Walter Shawcross	b Stretford
11667 L/Sgt John Henry Sheasby	b Chorlton on Medlock
31060 L/Cpl Leonard Shires	b and lived Leeds
26692 Pte Alfred Smith	b Manchester, lived Bradford, Mcr
11671 Pte James Willoughby Smith	b Salford
11674 Sgt Arthur Spencer	b Ryde, Isle of Wight, lived Stretford
12462 Sgt Ernest Spink	b Broughton
12215 Pte Thomas William Stretch	b Longsight
28865 L/Cpl Charles David Stuart	b Wigan, lived Wallingford, Berks
33840 Pte Harold Sutton	b Manchester, lived Withington
12695 Pte Arthur Swetnam	b Longton, Staffs, lived Stoke
11686 Pte Alfred Ernest Taylor	b Rusholme
11987 Pte Harold Thompson	b Newton Heath
26618 Pte William Henry Thornley	b St Helens
33849 Pte Harry Thrower	b Long Sutton, Lincs, lived Walthamstow
27621 Pte Percy Titley	b Manchester
12469 Pte Arthur Collins Tomlinson	b Rochdale
25016 Pte Arthur Turnbull	b Manchester
11689 Sgt Fred Turner	b and lived Bury
11692 Pte James Waters	b Pendleton
12481 Pte Cyril Watts	b Hulme
34184 Pte Alfred Webb	b Smallwood, Cheshire, lived Levenshulme
11768 Pte Albert Wilkinson	b Collyhurst
12243 Pte Cyril Rowe Willcocks	b Cardiff
11704 Pte Albert Williams	b Salford, lived Seedley
11960 Cpl Arthur Williams	b and lived Salford
12785 Pte Peter Williams	b Manchester, lived Salford
31031 Pte Alfred Willmott	b Manchester, lived Salford
11716 Pte John Wood	b Hulme
11970 Pte John Wood	b Salford, lived Seedley

Home at Last

On the Way

The parson asked if I felt fit to go before the Doctor and took me to see him. The Doctor looked at my wound and inoculated me in my right breast, then I was put on another motor to a place called Heilly. More tea and bread and butter, then before another doctor. Just as I got to him in his room, before he could speak, I shot outside again. I could feel myself falling. He ordered me to lie down a while and when he came to examine me he put another ticket on me with a "B" on it, meaning "Base". I stayed here until nearly midnight and then some of us were put on the train to no-one knew where. A nurse came and spoke English, the first English girl I had seen or heard speak since I left home.

We arrived at Rouen at 1.00pm on Monday, 24th July, and I was examined by another doctor who marked me "S", which meant "Ship" - England! A good sleep that night on a nice bed.

The next dinner time my name was called out, two tickets put on me and we had to get ready to go on the train. About 2.30pm we left Rouen, arriving at Le Havre about 7.00pm. On to the boat and I fell asleep very soon.

19th Manchesters

Casualties 23 - 29 July 1916

b = birthplace as listed in *Soldiers Died in the Great War*

KIA = Killed in Action. DoW = Died of Wounds

31071	Pte Victor Henderson	b Manchester *(died in UK)*	DoW 23 July
12382	Pte Geoffrey Knowles	b Birkdale, Southport	DoW 23 July
12548	Pte Charles Abbott	b Mobberley, lived Northwich	DoW 24 July
12090	L/Sgt Arnold Hague	b Hulme	KIA 25 July
12172	L/Cpl Leonard Parkin	b Queens Park, Manchester	DoW 27 July
12656	Pte William Lawton	b Miles Platting	DoW 28 July
31219	Pte John Wilde *(above)*	b Manchester, lived Irlam	DoW 29 July

26 Jul 1916: Next morning I asked if we were in England but the boat, the Asturias, had not moved. However, we sailed about 6.00am, arriving at Southampton about four that afternoon. Two hours later we were on the train, which took us to Rubery, near Birmingham. By 11.00pm we were travelling on motors to the hospital. People were cheering all along the roads, but I could hardly realise I was in England. A bath and into bed.

27 Jul 1916: Next morning the Sister came talking and asked me if I was also suffering from shell shock. I said no, but she said I would have to have something for my nerves. About 10.00am the Doctor came, examined my wound and explained to the Sister where the bullet had gone. Then he turned to me and said, "Have you been badly shaken at any time, near a mine, buried or anything like that?" I told him about the "coal box" near Trones Wood. They gave me some medicine and told me to keep in bed, not work my shoulder and keep quiet. I was in here until the end of August, then went on my ten days' sick leave.

Reunited

Sep 1916 - Aug 1917: During my sick leave I met my brother Tom, who had been wounded in Trones Wood, and after this I had to report to the Manchester

The hospital ship Asturias

Regiment depot at Ashton. My brother and I were here together, doing three marches a day of one hour each. He went before the Doctor, was marked C1 and sent to B Company, 3rd Manchesters, at Cleethorpes. A week later I paraded and was marked C1.

The Doctor said, "Wounded on 1st?"
"No," I said, "23rd."
"You were a lucky lad to last all that while in it. How many Germans did you kill?"
I said, "None. I might have hurt a few."
"I see, I see," he said. "You don't want to know."

The next day I came to the same Company and Battalion as Tom, the 3rd Manchesters, billeted in the Gas House, Cleethorpes Road, Grimsby. Here we did two marches of about one hour each per day.

After three weeks here about 80 of us were transferred to the 2nd Garrison Battalion, Lincoln Regiment, for Home Service. We went to Marsh Chapel, stayed here a week and our Company came to George Street Schools, Grimsby. Here we did guards and fatigues but generally had an easy time.

My brother got marked A1 in March and was sent back to the 3rd Manchesters at Cleethorpes. I was transferred to the 26th Durham Light Infantry Works Battalion and was telephone orderly at the ASC, George Street. In May 1917 I was transferred to the 7th Labour Battalion, in July to the 506th Works Company and now I have been ordered to move again. But I cannot complain, having had a good time in Grimsby and an easy time too. It has been my best time soldiering and I have enjoyed it. My brother has been kept in England on musketry, both of us having had a very good time and made good friends. We will both be sorry to leave.

Au Revoir

7 Aug 1917: My brother Tom and I have been here in Grimsby since last November, having a very good time playing billiards. I taught him to dance here and we have been dancing, meeting some very nice people and making a good

Albert Andrews in 1916

Manchester Regiment barracks *Ashton-under-Lyne*

many friends. My mother has visited us twice here, my dad once. We have just spent an enjoyable weekend together and I think my brother will endorse my statement that Grimsby is the finest place we have been in whilst soldiering and the people the kindest. There are a good many soldiers' clubs, the ladies giving up their time and pleasure to look after the soldiers. All I can say about the Grimsby people and their kindness is (what the French General said about our bravery), "Beyond praise."

Anyway, tomorrow, Wednesday 8th August 1917, 1 leave for Strensall, my brother Tom going on his draft leave ready to go out again. So will say au revoir to all our friends. So sorry to go leaving a nice place, good friends and a good time behind us. Such people as we have met in Grimsby are well worth fighting for.

Au revoir from a Manchester lad who has written this book of his experiences, telling the truth just as he can remember it occurring of what he has actually been through or seen. Other lads may have fared worse, some better, but this is my life in the Army up to the present date, 7th August 1917.

I am looking forward to my last night in Grimsby tonight, having spent last night and the weekend with my brother Tom. We have done three years' soldiering together, he being in France 13 days less than me. Tonight I am going to have supper with him and a great friend of ours, Dick Booth, then we are both off elsewhere tomorrow.

This is the first time we have been parted as soldiers but we are both smiling, both saying tonight the same thing: "We will never let them get us down." We are sorry to part after being together so long, but we are soldiers and orders are orders and must be obeyed.

When he returned to France, Tom Andrews served in the 2nd/5th Battalion XX The Lancashire Fusiliers. Near Ypres in September, they were moved to trenches at Lempire, south-east of Epehy and facing the St Quentin Canal and the outposts of the Hindenburg Line.

Passchendaele Ridge had been taken on 6th November and the British Commander-in-Chief was looking for an opportunity to strike a blow elsewhere while German troops were still heavily concentrated in the north. He also wanted to use his tanks, which by now had increased both in numbers and efficiency. He chose to attack near Cambrai and to mount simultaneous subsidiary actions which would distract the enemy's attention from the main assault. As part of this subsidiary action, the 2nd/5th LFs were ordered to attack a mound called the Knoll just south of Vendhuile.

Acting Corporal Tom Andrews was killed in this attack on 20th November 1917.

A postcard sent by Tom Andrews from the camp at Strensall, Yorkshire, in July 1917. Tom is in the centre of the back row